The A to Z of Chelsea
Where Were You When We Were
Shocking?

D1421635

Neil L. Smith

The A to Z of Chelsea
Where Were You When We Were Shocking?
Copyright Neil L. Smith 2018
ISBN: 978-1721911561
First published by Gate 17 2018

Cover design: Gate 17
www.gate17.co.uk

This book is dedicated to my Wife
Cheryl

In Memory of
Steve Vest
19/12/56 – 23/2/2012

CONTENTS

FOREWORD

This short work is a selection of my memories from just a few of the now in excess of 2000 Chelsea matches I have attended. It is also I suppose, a look back at some of the occurrences I have witnessed that in some way have shaped my life.

My first game was at Stamford Bridge in 1966 when Chelsea beat West Ham 6-2 on April 9th when I attended with my older brother Martin.

When I got home after that game, I wrote some words about the day and it was the start of a habit that, as I got older, became a diary.

If you're a patron of the Chelsea fanzine *cfcuk*, you might well have previously read some of what is contained in *The A-Z of Chelsea WWYWWWS?.*

However, those submissions to *cfcuk* were in fact abridged versions of my original musings, cut short because of the wordage allowance set by the fanzine.

Indeed, the following pages are full and accurate transcriptions taken from the diary I have kept recounting every Chelsea match I have attended.

Following Chelsea as a season-ticket holder and also as a domestic and European supporter over many years has given me some of the most pleasurable and memorable memories of my life.

Yes, plenty have been sweetened with the taste of a glorious end to a successful campaign but many - indeed, the overwhelming majority - are cherished moments with some great friends I've made amongst the fantastic Chelsea support.

I hope you enjoy what you'll read but, more importantly, enjoy your time following Chelsea Football Club.

ACKNOWLEDGEMENTS

My sincere and grateful thanks go to Mark Worrall for publishing this book on his now renowned Gate 17 label. It's a massive honour for me to have been allowed to publish a work in my 'own right' and I hope you'll find it up to the high standards that Mark always sets for anything he allows Gate 17 to put to market.

My first 'contribution' to the literary world came when I was fortunate enough to have been a co-author of *Eddie Mac Eddie Mac*, another title in the Gate 17 catalogue, alongside Mark, Kelvin Barker, Mark Meehan and David Johnstone.

WWYWWWS? would never have seen the light of day had it not been for the massive help David has been in not only encouraging me to first publish some of my accounts in the *cfcuk* Chelsea fanzine but also in persuading me after many years of cajoling to put this collection of memoirs to print. Added to that, David's help in the overall production of *WWYWWWS?* has been invaluable.

Finally, a massive thanks to all the Chelsea supporters mentioned in the book and also to my many friends who I've met along the road following Chelsea Football Club - thank you for travelling with me, the journey's been fantastic... you know who you are.

Neil L. Smith

Aston Villa 2 Chelsea 0
18th April 1978

Football League Division One
Villa Park
Chelsea; Peter Bonetti, Graham Wilkins, Ron Harris, Ian Britton, David Hay, Steve Wicks, Steve Finnieston, Ken Swain, Tommy Langley, Ray Lewington, Lee Frost (Bill Garner 75)
Booked; Britton, Wilkins
Manager; Ken Shellito
Referee; Alex Lees
Attendance; 27,375

Worryingly it's now seven games since our last victory, a 3-1 home win over European Cup holders Liverpool.

I am making my first ever visit to Villa Park, travelling on the British Rail football special departing Euston 12.10pm and arriving at Witton 14.05pm.

The mood in the station buffet pre-boarding is a lot darker than 12 months ago when Chelsea were on the verge of returning to the First Division and playing some superb football along the way.

Indeed, the corresponding weekend a year ago before a 2-1 win over promotion rivals Nottingham Forest was deemed a defining moment in attaining that success.

Today, Forest are remarkably sitting at the top of the table entertaining Leeds United and upon the cusp of their greatest ever achievement.

Taking my seat on the train, I could feel the sombre atmosphere which was probably not helped with the new alcohol ban being strictly adhered to!

Having been late to bed the night before after enjoying the music of the British Afro-rock band, Osibisa at Skindles, Maidenhead I decide it may be best to have forty winks.

I think back to Chelsea's last visit to Villa Park for a league fixture in September 1966. Amazingly, the two clubs have not met since then due to a mixture of fortunes.

On that day, a nine year old boy sat beside his transistor radio fishing in the River Colne at Cowley Middlesex and in between landing several gudgeon, each weighing two or three ounces, noisily celebrated after hearing of his team's 6-2 victory.

Returning home, and after admitting that he had not taken his father's advice to use bread paste instead of maggots to tempt a decent bream, he learned that Bobby Tambling had netted five of Chelsea's six that afternoon.

His elder brother then teased him that, being only nine and not 12, he would not be allowed to stay up until 10.25pm to watch the highlights on BBC *Match of the Day*.

However after tea and *Doctor Who*, Mother relented and announced that as Bobby's feat was bordering on historic, the 9pm curfew would be waived on this occasion.

Kenneth Wolstenholme's commentary that night highlighted that the Chelsea followers in front of him were regaling in victory by singing *Strolling* as he pointed out that was what their team were doing, strolling onto victory.

Before departing for bed, the tired siblings hear Wolstenholme refer to young Johnnie Boyle as a "cheeky monkey" when beating his opponent twice on the byline before putting Bobby in for his fifth.

The only outstanding matter as they climbed the stairs was whether the team were wearing white shirts or the new Swedish yellow they had read about?

Alighting at Witton Station, the Chelsea contingent are frogmarched unceremoniously around to the visitors' entrance.

We are 400 strong but, when passing the Aston Hall public house adjacent to the ground, a sizeable number of aggressors seek a confrontation. The situation is suitably policed but concerns me when pondering the return excursion.

After entering the ground, we learn that Chelsea are to give a debut to 20 year old Lee Frost who replaces Clive Walker on the left wing.

Scottish International David Hay, having missed most of the present campaign through injury, will wear the number five shirt and resume his partnership with Steve Wicks which had proved so successful last term.

Today Chelsea are wearing an all yellow kit. I am aware that, being superstitious, the strip has only witnessed one victory this season, a remarkable 5-4 win at Birmingham on New Years Eve when Tommy Langley notched a 'perfect hat-trick' – one with the right, one with the left and one with his head.

Villa proceed to have the lion's share of the play with the 36 year old Peter Bonetti keeping the game scoreless at half time. Frost has had Chelsea's lone effort at goal a dipping shot from some 25 yards just clearing the crossbar at the Holte End.

Local hero Andy Gray is giving fellow Scotsman Hay a torrid time culminating in a booking for our man and, when Gordan Cowans nets on the hour, the writing is on the wall for us.

Ray Wilkins also tries his luck from some 35 yards but when Wicks glances a corner past his own keeper the Chelsea hordes head for the exit.

Having been uncomfortable with proceedings upon arrival, I suggest to my travelling companion that we too should perhaps beat a retreat. His optimism is boundless though and he insists on seeing the last three minutes out assuring me that those departing will not be allowed to exit the ground en masse.

However, approaching the final whistle the visitors' enclosure is sparsely occupied and I note that a faction gathered adjacent to us over the separating wall are gesturing that we may be seeing them soon outside.

My fears of trepidation are well founded when, within 20 yards of the ground, I receive a haymaker to the back of the head and race off back towards Witton Station where thankfully we regroup and are on our way in a few minutes.

Arguments ensue on the way home. Some about the replacement of Walker with Frost but moreover those who fled from their opposing numbers.

Obtaining a copy of the *Evening News* when I arrive back at Euston, I read there is further bad news in that fellow strugglers West Ham have defeated Derby 3-0 and QPR have beaten high flying Coventry City 2-1.

We lie 18th with five games remaining. Villa are up to tenth and Forest are four points clear at the top.

Next week we entertain Wolves who are in the bottom three just one point below us.

Desperate Days.

Bristol Rovers 3 Chelsea 0
23rd February 1980

Football League Division Two
Eastville
Chelsea; Bob Iles, Gary Locke, Dennis Rofe, Tommy Langley, Colin Pates, Gary Chivers, Ian Britton, Mike Fillery, Lee Frost, Clive Walker, Ron Harris
Sub Not Used; 12 Mike Nutton
Manager; Geoff Hurst
Referee; Jeff Bray
Attendance; 14,176

Chelsea are presently third in the Second Division and have recently experienced mixed fortunes.

A couple of weeks ago, we went down 2-4 at home to Shrewsbury Town but then enjoyed a 3-2 victory at Watford, a team also fancied for promotion.

Today we are heading off down the M4 to play Bristol Rovers who we have already beaten 1-0 at home and lie near the foot of the table.

Bill's driving over from Walton in his Ford Granada and picking up Gary at Sunbury before we mob up with the Hayes and Uxbridge boys in Mick's new Ford Escort Mexico and head west.

There are two car loads and we are nine strong.

I chanced my arm by writing to the home club a while ago enclosing an open cheque and requesting stand seats. To everyone's surprise, the tickets have arrived and we will be able to quaff an extra ale or two before sauntering into the Eastville Stadium at about 2.45pm.

Taking up our positions, I survey the surroundings. Eastville reminds me a little of Stamford Bridge as it was when I first visited in the mid-60s.

It has a perimeter track for greyhound racing and the home terrace is suitably called the Tote End.

Perusing the team line-ups in the programme in conjunction with the Tannoy announcements, we learn that our regular goalkeeper Petar Borota is absent and will be replaced by Bob Iles.

I inform my companions that my cousin, Jim from Poole in Dorset, had phoned recently excited by the news of Iles' signing for £10,000 from Weymouth as he was a fellow cricketer and able wicketkeeper to boot and that there was every chance he may provide complimentary tickets in the future.

Chelsea are also giving a debut to veteran left back Dennis Rofe having signed from Leicester.

We agree after some head scratching that Rofe was in the Orient side which inflicted a shock 3-2 5th Round FA Cup defeat in 1972, one of the darkest afternoons in our time following the club.

The following Saturday saw us defeated in the League Cup Final by unfancied Stoke City at Wembley and. in many eyes, it was the end of an era which would soon see the likes of Peter Osgood and Alan Hudson departing the

Bridge.

Glancing down the Rovers eleven I note Terry Cooper, another veteran, at left back.

I have better memories than of Rofe's appearance against us.

In the 1970 FA Cup Final replay at Old Trafford with time running out and the boys still a goal down Peter Bonetti twice had to make outstanding saves from the marauding Cooper in the white of our nemesis Leeds United.

The rest, as they say, is history.

A local informs me as the teams take to the pitch that we should observe the home number ten, Garry Mabbutt, "A really good prospect, unlike that Tony Pulis at eleven".

The omens are not good though and I am not in favour of the yellow and green 'Norwich' kit preferring the red, white and green which we sported last time here in a 2-1 victory when Teddy Maybank netted a fine goal when racing through from the halfway line, before Ian Hutchinson added another.

Soon after the break, Shaun Penny nets his second before the aforementioned Pulis hits a screamer from all of 30 yards. 3-0 to Rovers.

Looking to our left, we survey skirmishes between Chelsea hooligans and the local constabulary before a perimeter wall collapses and 100s of youths are scrambling around behind the goal.

As the final whistle sounds, the disorder is still escalating and we endure the wrath of the home fans around us.

Over the pre-match lunch, I had made the mistake of letting my travelling companions know that it would suit me to head straight home after the game as my relatively new girl friend wished to introduce me to her parents over dinner.

'Ginger', in particular, was not in agreement with such an itinerary and has brought to the lads' attention a selection of watering holes in hamlets such as Marlborough (Wiltshire) and Wantage (Oxfordshire) from the *Good Beer Guide* which accompanies him on every excursion.

And so to Marlborough, where we find ourselves sampling the local fare when a group of Villa fans returning from the south coast challenge us to a singalong around a grand piano.

The governor looks non too pleased but agrees that we can continue provided someone can genuinely master the ivories as well as the high notes without upsetting his regulars.

I manage to complete the first few bars of *Strangers In The Night* (Frank Sinatra) before Ginge begins belting out *My Girl* (Madness) with hastily prepared new lyrics to fit the occasion.

"She doesn't want me to watch Chelsea etc etc", a taunt aimed in my direction.

We are then asked to vacate the premises and it's fast approaching 8pm.

Back in the Ford Granada, Bill senses my anxiety – will I be back in Maidenhead for the get together?

"She'll be OK, just phone her," he says.

He then points at what looks like a car battery the size of a house brick by the gearstick.

"What on earth is that?" I enquire.
"A mobile phone…"

I decline the offer with Steve and Tony giggling like schoolgirls in the back seats.

It's then on to Wantage where we then find ourselves in the White Horse and accepting another challenge, this time around pub games.

It's getting on for 10pm and the bar billiards final still hasn't been completed.

Furthermore, there is an unexpected treat of bowls of chips and sandwiches to cause further distraction.

Back in the car at closing time, Bill reassures me again, "She'll be fine – you're a good bloke but I wouldn't ring her now though but tomorrow first thing. Say we broke down on the M4 and you couldn't get to a phone but didn't want to worry her."

Back home in Buckinghamshire at around 1am after numerous pee and puke stops, I retire to bed and contemplate the following day.

Yes… Bill's right. I'll ring her first thing or after I have played for my Sunday morning football team, had a few pints with the boys and devoured Mum's Sunday roast.

She'll be fine.

Carlisle United 2 Chelsea 1
20th October 1982

Football League Division Two
Brunton Park
Chelsea; Steve Francis, Gary Locke, Chris Hutchings, Colin Pates, Micky Droy, Joey Jones, Clive Walker, John Bumstead, Bryan Robson (Colin Lee), David Speedie, Peter Rhoades-Brown
Scorer; Lee 82
Booked; Jones
Sent Off; Jones
Manager; John Neal
Referee; Robert Dixon
Attendance; 7,141

We are heading north from Euston on the London to Glasgow Express, en-route to Cumbria for the season's longest jaunt,

It's worth paying a little bit extra to avoid the British Rail rolling stock and face a day being herded like cattle.

There are about 20 of us travelling with Chelsea Supporters Club whose stalwart historian and travel officer, Ron Hockings, advises that good behaviour is of paramount importance and that the alcohol ban is to be strictly adhered to. Indeed, disappointingly there is no buffet car,

Taking up our reserved seats on the train there is the usual banter.

Those who did not make the midweek trek to Merseyside where Chelsea successfully defended their first leg 3-1 lead in the League Cup against the mighty Tranmere Rovers are the butt of the flak flying around.

Two goals from the veteran, Bryan 'Pop' Robson saw the Blues return victorious winning 5-2 upon aggregate.

Thankfully, I am excluded from the jibes as I invented a dental appointment the previous Wednesday and endured the British Rail special to Rock Ferry returning at around 2.30am.

Back in the office on Thursday morning, I explained my subdued demeanour as being down to the numbing injection received during the treatment received.

As the journey unfolds, I recommend to my travelling companions that when we alight at Carlisle we sheepishly head for the toilets allowing the bulk of the passengers to disperse then casually venture off into the city centre for a hearty lunch.

Unfortunately and despite being law abiding citizens, we know from experience that there is every chance that we will be apprehended by the local constabulary and frogmarched straight to Brunton Park should we be identified as football supporters.

It is a sad indictment of present times. We are all 'tarred with the same brush'.

The plan is put into action.

A police officer with a loud hailer announces that all

Chelsea followers should congregate on the left and await further instruction.

Emerging ten minutes later from the public conveniences, I tell the lads to keep their heads down and "look normal!"

Just as I think we are in the clear, the long arm of the law descends upon me and a constable obstructs my path inviting me to join an assembled band to the left of the station concourse.

I try to appear dumbfounded and plead that I am not a football follower but due to attend my brother's wedding for which I am running late.

I then fail the initiative test.

"What is your brother's address, where is he getting married, what's his intended bride's name, where is your suit?"

Upon then being asked for I.D. and producing my drivers licence, Mr Plod espies my match ticket.

Bang to rights, I now join the chain gang and I am told that I will be put under particular surveillance.

Nearing the stadium I point out to our captors that we need to leave the escort and move towards the main stand where our seats are allocated.

After some discussion, the officer in charge decides that this will not be possible and that we will have to enter the terrace behind a goal designated for the visitors and contact the club for a refund by post next week!

We are already crestfallen an hour before kick-off!

Then there is a commotion a few 100 yards behind us with baying youths exchanging curses and oathes. This diverts the constabulary's attention and they take flight.

We take our chance and the four of us just run and run... and run towards some waste land at that end of the ground down an embankment and over a small brook, thereby disturbing a lone angler.

There's a building in sight in which we seek sanctuary. It's a golf club and surprisingly we make our way in, brush ourselves down and order some drinks.

No interrogation here. We are made quite welcome. In fact the angler joins us and remarks how fit we must be or just desperate for a drink.

After sampling the local fare, we join the crowd heading for the match and take our rightful seats.

This is my first visit to Carlisle and I turn my mind back to another League Cup tie in 1969 when I remember, as I delivered the morning newspapers, the headline upon the back page that read, "BRAVE BONETTI CANNOT SAVE CHELSEA!"

First Division Chelsea had been humbled by the second tier Cumbrians 1-0 against all odds.

However, the main story revolved around Chelsea goalkeeper Bonetti being rendered unconscious when struck upon the head by a granite slate launched from the terrace.

Still dazed, he was beaten by a 35 yard shot from right back Derek Hemstead.

The newspaper went on to include the words of Kevin Howley, the referee, who addressed the crowd over the Tannoy whilst our brave custodian received treatment;

"I am not going to abandon the match no matter what the score is but I'll empty the ground if there is any more trouble and then finish the game."

I wondered how many of the 18,500 that witnessed events upon that evening were in attendance today.

Perusing down the line-ups in the match programme, I do not recognise any of the players appearing in the blue shirts of the hosts.

The breaking news for Chelsea though is that Welsh international Joey Jones has completed his transfer from Wrexham and will line up alongside Micky Droy at centre back wearing the number 6 shirt. There are mixed feelings amongst our group upon receiving this news.

After 20 minutes having been played, I become acquainted with the names of Malcolm Poskett and Alan Shoulder as both find the net for the home side as we enter the break two goals down.

At half time the match announcer informs us over the Tannoy that the attendance of 7,141 is the largest of the season so far.

Upon the hour, things become even worse when our debutant international is dismissed after a series of rash challenges.

Centre forward Colin Lee then replaces Pop Robson and soon finds the net for the ten men but it's too little too late. Another defeat and we remain 12th in the Second

Division.

Travelling back on the train the inquest begins and I recall a recent meeting arranged at quite short notice midweek in a conference room in the East Stand at Stamford Bridge.

The gathering had been conveyed to welcome the new chairman, Kenneth Bates, and team manager, John Neal into the club and provide an insight as to their collective plans for the future,

A question and answer session descended into a slanging match with one burly middle aged attendee labelling Mr Bates a cowboy and Mr Neal a clown.

His parting shot at the manager had been around the likelihood of Joey Jones being signed.

John Neal replied, "He's coming and you will love him!"

Ken Bates closed the evening by retorting that he would saddle up and head back to his ranch!

I put the defeat down to the absence of our best player, Micky Fillery, who was ruled out by injury.

Trying to raise spirits before arriving back in London, I pointed out our progress through the previous round of the League Cup and the forthcoming tie at Notts County in ten days time.

I fancy our chances although they are in the top flight whilst we are languishing in the second.

Yes – I fancy us to pull off yet another giant killing – can't wait.

Dundalk 2 Chelsea 3
2nd August 1986

Martin Lawler Testimonial
Tolka Park
Chelsea; Tony Godden, Darren Wood (Doug Rougvie), Colin Pates, John Bumstead (John McNaught), Joe McLaughlin, Steve Wicks, Pat Nevin, Keith Jones, Kerry Dixon, David Speedie (Roy Wegerle), Mickey Hazard (Gordon Durie)
Manager; John Hollins
Referee; Paddy Daly
Attendance; Unknown

We will follow the Chelsea over land and sea...

How many times must I have joined in that refrain although never actually having crossed any ocean partaking in my favourite pastime?

Well, a trip to Southern Ireland for a long weekend taking in fixtures with Dundalk and EMFA Kilkenny will give me that accreditation and some bragging rights back in Blighty at the start of the new season.

I meet up with travelling companions, Steve and Tony, at Heathrow on Friday afternoon excited by the prospect of their excellent camaraderie and the ensuing 'craic'.

Whilst Steve and I have secured our flight tickets, Tony, as a British Airways employee, is to travel on 'standby' (gratis) and will be on the flight after us at 5pm.

Our descent into Dublin is a turbulent one thanks to the accompaniment of a violent thunderstorm. Once down, we secure the hire of a Ford Fiesta for the weekend and then check the status of Tony's flight.

We now learn that Dublin Airport is to shut down due to the storm. There is confusion as to where our colleague's plane has been routed. Initially, we are informed it is to be diverted to Bradford/Leeds and then Knock on the north west Irish coast.

We finally receive confirmation that it will land in Knock. Upon enquiry, we are then told that the passengers will endure a four hour coach journey to Dublin.

We return to the tourist information desk to book accommodation and stress that cheap and cheerful is the order of the day.

"I'll ring Mrs McDonagh on the Howth Road," our genial receptionist informs us.

Indeed, chez McDonagh are able to provide three beds in one room – no problem.

Upon making Mrs McDonagh's acquaintance, we explain our colleague's predicament and that we will have to return to Dublin City Centre coach station to hopefully locate him (due in around midnight) then return to her hostelry.

Mrs McDonagh then points to a crucifix above our bedroom door and announces,

"Now you are not to bring any women back here!"

Upon departing for the coach station, a local outside Mrs McDonagh's enquires as to the ownership of the Ford

Fiesta. We inform him it is upon hire from Hertz.

"Well I would not leave it at the front here when you get back, If you do it may be there in the morning but the wheels wont".

Finding the coach station and obtaining a progress report as to the whereabouts of the diverted passengers, we learn that they are scheduled to arrive after midnight,

Steve and I take refuge in a popular crowded bar and make light of the trip thus far over a couple of glasses of the old "Liffey water". This is my first taste of the proper Dublin Guinness as opposed to the Park Royal brand I enjoy at home. It's different to be sure.

Indeed, the craic is good as you would expect on a Friday evening in the centre of Dublin and we begin to relax a little.

A telephone on the bar rings and the publican booms out, "Is there a Paddy Murphy here?"

We burst into raucous laughter but those around us do not seem to see anything funny in this interlude.

"Dumb limeys…" we hear muttered.

Tony is soon located and we head back to the Howth Road B&B,

Mrs McD greets us and forewarns of a full Irish breakfast like no other in the morning.

Upon retiring, I find that, much to Steve and Tony's amusement, my bed is more akin to a hammock but given the afternoon and evening's events I'm soon away.

In the morning, the full Irish is heartily devoured and we compliment Mrs McD, but what on earth is soda bread?

Tony takes to the wheel and we head north up the east coast towards Dundalk. I'm navigating thanks to a map and there's no rush as it's an evening kick-off at 7pm.

The only traffic congestion encountered is that of sheep and their herders.

A few hours must have passed as we have heard Bruce Hornsby and the Range "The Way It Is" played at least three times on the station we're listening to on the car radio.

At around 5pm, we settle in a roadside inn and check our bearings. The walls are covered in black and white photos of local Gaelic football teams.

The landlord notes our interest and asks about our itinerary.

We proudly proclaim that we are on our way to watch our team play Dundalk in a pre-season friendly.

"You know it's at Tolka and not Oriel Park?" he asks us.

We thank him for the advice before venturing off.

Arriving in Dundalk and locating their home ground at around 6pm. we are a little surprised as to both the ease of parking and also the lack of people.

A gentleman approaches the Fiesta and enquires as to the purpose of our stay.

When we mention the fixture he reiterates that the venue

is Tolka Park.

"Is it far?" we enquire.
"Yes... it's in Dublin." He replies.

The penny drops as to the information provided by the landlord of the inn.

A quick decision is made to bomb it back to Dublin where we may at least catch part of the game.

An hour and a half later we are back in Dublin after a day sightseeing. Luckily, Tolka Park is soon located and we leg it to the ground and view proceedings.

Strangely, expecting it to be nearing the interval, the teams are just emerging and upon enquiring we learn that the kick-off has been delayed due to the non-appearance of the referee.

Somewhat comically, we then see that Chelsea's Scottish international, Doug Rougvie, is to run the line until hopefully an accredited official is located.

Looking around the crowd, I note some familiar faces from London and locals sporting Chelsea blue joining their throng and beginning to trot out some of our anthems.

On the pitch, Dundalk are running around like men possessed and I am fearful that this fixture is to be very competitive and hope that we do not incur any serious injuries with the new season approaching.

On the terracing, it is apparent that a band of our followers have recently returned from watching England at the World Cup in Mexico. One of their songs regales, *Drink all day in Monterray*, a reference to where most of the

English camped out and imbibed.

Unfortunately, a faction from behind one goal move toward the group and begin chanting, *Who put the ball in the England net? Diego, Diego, Diego Maradona!*

Fists and bottles fly and we take cover pitch side. The local youngsters actually allay our fears by announcing that the Garda will have things under control in no time and indeed so it proves!

A few ejections later and all eyes are back on the pitch.

Chelsea take control with goals from John Bumstead and Keith Jones providing a half time lead. However, with Rougvie relieved of linesman duties Dundalk storm back to level with only minutes remaining.

However the final twist sees Kerry Dixon net with a trade mark header and it appears everyone is content with the commitment of both sides in an enthralling game.

Back to the B&B ,with four wheels on our wagon, we tuck into another McDonagh culinary offering of bacon and cabbage pie. Delicious. Furthermore Mrs McD then witnesses us make love to copious pints of the black stuff and has no worries as to our intentions.

Tomorrow we head south to Kilkenny having now secured our fourth win on tour following victories over Caernarfon (3-0) Bangor City (4-0) and an Anglesey X1 (1-0).

Yes it's looking good ahead of our opening fixture with Norwich City at Stamford Bridge on 23rd August.

Bring it on!

Everton 3 Chelsea 2
11th November 1978

Football League Division One
Goodison Park
Chelsea; John Phillips, Graham Wilkins, David Stride, Garry Stanley, Steve Wicks, Ron Harris, Duncan McKenzie, Ray Wilkins, Tommy Langley, Ken Swain, Clive Walker
Sub Not Used; Ian Britton
Scorers; McKenzie 9, Langley 48
Manager; Ken Shellito
Referee; Alan Jenkins
Attendance; 38,694

Ron Hockings has kindly agreed that we may join his travelling party of the Chelsea Supporters Club at Watford Junction today which is great for those of us travelling from Iver as it is nearer to home than Euston and easier to park.

Upon the platform there is a mixture of both Chelsea and Everton followers in around equal numbers. As we embark we find that two carriages are reserved for CSC and ESCLA (Everton Supporters Club London Area).

The Everton contingent are in fine fettle as their team remain unbeaten in the opening 13 games lying two points behind leaders Liverpool in second place.

Chelsea are in 20th place and have not won on the road since their first away game, a midweek 1-0 victory at

27

Wolverhampton Wanderers who are one spot below us in the table with Birmingham City bottom.

Mingling in the buffet car, the exiled Evertonians are quick to remind the travelling true Blues of their last visit to Goodison Park some six months previously when Chelsea were trounced 6-0.

It was April 29th 1978, eight years to the day that Chelsea recorded their first FA Cup success beating Leeds 2-1 in a replay at Old Trafford. Remarkably, Peter Bonetti and Ron Harris who collected winners' medals were still playing in this struggling team.

There were only three games remaining and relegation to the Second Division was still a distinct possibility in our first season back in the top flight.

Everton were looking to secure second position and, furthermore, the game was given extra scrutiny as their number nine, England International Bob' Latchford, had already notched 28 league goals.

The *Daily Express* had offered £10,000 to any player to score thirty goals in a season so many observers believed that there was every chance that Latchford would complete that feat with a brace on the day.

And so it proved! Although he didn't find the net until the 72nd minute, he then netted a dubiously awarded penalty ten minutes from time to complete the rout with hundreds of fans invading the pitch in celebration.

Quite comically, after the initial invasion had been quelled, an elderly Evertonian with a walking cane finally reached Latchford in the centre circle to offer his congratulations.

We had returned to Lime Street Station somewhat crestfallen but were soon bouyed by the news that Liverpool's 2-0 win at West Ham had ensured our First Division status for another year at least.

Back in the buffet car, there's also talk around the possibility of revenge attacks by Merseyside gangs on Chelsea supporters following on from trouble at the reverse fixture between the clubs at the opening day fixture.

On that afternoon, a tube train of visiting fans returning to Euston had been ambushed at High Street Kensington underground station resulting in complete pandemonium with the fighting spilling onto the tracks and escapees fleeing down the tunnels. With all electricity to the rail lines being suspended the network was brought to a standstill for at least an hour.

Alighting in Liverpool, we jump into a black cab and request that we go straight to Goodison Park.

When the cabbie asks if we've been to the city before, we know to answer in the affirmative and will not require an expensive sight seeing tour.

When the teams are announced, both line-ups are almost identical to those last April.

As well as including chief tormentors Latchford, Andy King and Dave Thomas, the Everton team also has two other names which stick in the craw.

Left back is Mike Pejic, formerly of Stoke City. I recall that in the first half of the League Cup Final of 1972 he committed two fouls upon Chris Garland when our man was well placed and, in my mind, he should have been sent to the stands.

As I've commented before, that game was deemed to be 'the beginning of the end'.

There's also Martin Dobson wearing the number 8 shirt. I remember attending the Chelsea versus Burnley FA Cup 4th round tie in 1970 when goals from John Hollins and Peter Osgood had looked to see us through to the next round before the young Dobson netted twice in the last ten minutes to secure a replay.

However, a happier outcome this time as Chelsea then returned from Turf Moor victorious after Peter Houseman inspired an extra time win after we had trailed to a first half effort from Ralph Coates. The rest...

The Chelsea team includes recent signing from Everton, Duncan McKenzie, a maverick forward already to have served Nottingham Forest and Leeds before arriving at Goodison and being moved on by manager Gordon Lee.

Duncan is still loved by the Goodison faithful despite Lee's insistence that his showboating did not suit the style of play he was promoting.

The game kicks off and a repeat of last season's drubbing looks very possible with Chelsea keeper John Phillips called into action several times in the first ten minutes.

However, with a quarter hour played, Ray Wilkins finds McKenzie wide on the left with a superb forty yard pass. Our Duncan then sets off on a mazy cross-field dribble leaving three defenders in his wake before firing past Scottish international goalkeeper George Wood from all of 25 yards.

Amazingly, the goal is acclaimed by both sets of supporters. The Evertonians assembled at the Gwladys Street End launch into a refrain, *Gordon is a moron!,* a number presently occupying the charts by a performer named 'Jilted John'. It is a jibe at their manager for selling their favourite.

Our joy however is short lived, as the lively King soon races through for an equaliser.

Level at half time, our eyes are diverted to the paddock terrace below our lofty position in the top tier. A baying home mob have taken up position adjacent to the visiting supporters in the Stanley Park End but are separated by the Merseyside Constabulary.

Missiles begin to hail down onto the Chelsea contingent who move backwards to the refreshment shed. Some planks are removed from that building and a golf ball projected from the home louts is suitably repelled back into their number from a makeshift cudgel.

Minutes into the second half and somewhat surprisingly, Chelsea are ahead. Ray Wilkins puts Tommy Langley away and he finishes in style.

Again however, it's backs to the wall with Steve Wicks keeping last season's local hero Latchford at bay.

My 1970 nightmare is relived though when Martin Dobson nets with two headers to return the lead to the hosts.

With no sign of the disturbances below abating, we decide to beat an early retreat and hopefully find a passing cab back to Lime Street when the unthinkable happens.

Young Langley sprints through to net an apparent

equaliser but our celebrations are cut short when an errant linesman raises his flag after the referee had signalled a goal.

It's ruled out.

Our protestations have been noted by the home support and we are hotly pursued on leaving the ground. Thankfully though we only receive verbal abuse and find a bus back to the station.

Travelling back down south, we learn that we still occupy 20th position after bottom club Birmingham have recorded their first victory a 5-1 thrashing of mid-table Manchester United.

A lot of the talk is around Duncan McKenzie's excellent goal and the rumour circulating that former Chelsea legend Peter Osgood may soon be returning from exile in Philadelphia to accompany him upfront.

I can't believe that.

On an optimistic note however, I feel that our young left back David Stride has a most promising future ahead of him.

Looking along the carriage I catch sight of a TV soap character. I am sure that it is the bloke who plays Gordon Clegg in *Coronation Street*.

Indeed, a gentleman adjacent confirms that he's name is Bill Kenwright and, like himself, he travels to all Everton games from London.

We talk about the game and our different fortunes and soon we are nearing London. He compliments Butch

Wilkins and mentions that he should soon be an England captain.

I tell him that I can't understand how both Martin Dobson and Andy King have been consistently overlooked by the England selectors.

As we part company and bade each other well we acquaint ourselves.

"Thank you for your kind comments. My name's Bill King – I'm Andy's dad."

It's Spurs at home next week – a must win game.

I wonder if those Osgood rumours are true and the saviour of Stamford Bridge will be back in blue soon.

Fulham 1 Chelsea 1
2nd April 1983

Football League Division Two
Craven Cottage
Chelsea; Bob Iles, Joey Jones, Chris Hutchings, Colin Lee, Micky Droy, Colin Pates, Mike Fillery, John Bumstead, David Speedie, Peter Rhoades-Brown, Paul Canoville
Sub Not Used; Alan Mayes
Scorer; Canoville 19
Manager; John Neal
Referee; David Axcell
Attendance; 15,249

Having recently exited the FA Cup in the 4th round 1-2 at Derby, all that remains of the season are nine league games.

Today we make the short trip to Craven Cottage. We lie 14th in the Second Division whereas our neighbours occupy third place on 58 points, five behind second placed Wolves and ten behind leaders QPR.

As the top three now obtain automatic promotion, and with Leicester seven points behind Fulham, there looks a strong possibility that two west London sides will be in the First Division next season.

Our chairman, Ken Bates, commented on this likelihood in his programme notes last week and that the only way we would be able to compete for spectators with two top tier clubs upon our doorstep would be by sustaining a strong promotion challenge with "proper entertainment".

We meet up in our usual watering hole for home games, the Duke of Cumberland, on the New Kings Road, and try not to dwell on the previous week's 0-3 home defeat to Barnsley.

Instead, we discuss memorable games with Fulham at Craven Cottage. My brother Martin mentions that he saw history made in 1965 when John Boyle became our first ever player to appear as substitute when replacing George Graham in a 3-0 victory.

Indeed, the following season saw Tony Hateley, Chelsea's first £100,000 signing, score twice in a 3-1 win in front of 43,259 spectators – a record attendance.

More recently, I remember our visit upon Good Friday 1977 when we were chasing promotion and arrived in second place only to be humbled 3-1. George Best netted Fulham's second that day and ex-Arsenal hatchet man, Peter Storey, effectively nobbled Ray Lewington within seconds of the kick-off.

A clever move on their part as they had worked out the importance of Ray's role in the side whereby he would collect the ball in the middle of the park and then move it onto Ray Wilkins or Garry Stanley to set up our attacks.

In 1980, the last time they played here, Chelsea arrived topping the table and recorded a 2-1 victory with both goals coming from Clive Walker. A few days later though we were thrashed 5-1 at Birmingham and at the end of the season missed out on promotion finishing in fourth position.

It still sticks in the craw that, two days after West Ham beat Arsenal in the FA Cup Final, they travelled by coach to Roker Park and suffered a 2-0 defeat which secured Sunderland's promotion.

A win for the Irons would have seen Chelsea and not Sunderland promoted. Furthermore, this was the last season where only two points and not three were awarded for a victory.

If the new points system had been applied that season Chelsea, with 23 victories and seven draws, as opposed to the Makems 21wins and ten draws, would have gone up with a points total of 76 versus 73.

We stroll down to the Cottage and have the last pint in the Crabtree behind the Hammersmith End.

Sharon Duce and Ray Brooks, currently starring in the acclaimed TV drama 'Big Deal', are holding court at the bar and are celebrity Fulham fans. Ms Duce is successful in obtaining my agreement to donate £1 per week to the Save Fulham FC campaign by standing order.

Taking up our seats in the Stevenage Road Stand, I note that our former servant Lewington will wear the number 11 shirt for our hosts and wonder if any special instructions to contain him have been provided by manager John Neal to his players.

Chelsea's number 11 is young Paul Canoville, the first black player to appear for the first team when debuting at Crystal Palace the previous April.

I have followed Canoville's progress with great interest. I first saw him at Hillingdon Borough and was very pleased to see him then join Chelsea and appear regularly for the youth team on Saturday mornings at the Imperial Service Grounds in Harlington.

A couple of weeks ago, Paul netted twice, his first goals for the first team, in a 4-2 home win over Carlisle United in front of a paltry attendance of 6,677.

I overhear some dissenting voices around me when our team is announced and the number 11 position is made known.

There is a faction among our following who do not wish to make Paul, or indeed any other black player, welcome in the team.

When Paul appeared as substitute at Crystal Palace last April, his introduction and time on the playing field was punctuated with hoots of derision from some of the Chelsea contingent assembled there.

The game kicks off and despite the difference in league positions it is Chelsea who are creating the better chances with Mike Fillery looking particularly menacing and behind most of our best movements.

On 20 minutes, a corner from Mike is glanced on by Micky Droy and Canoville swivels and meets the ball with a supreme volley which screams into the Putney End net.

The goal is suitably celebrated upon the terrace behind but not by some assembled around us.

People around me are starting to argue about the 'merits' of black players turning out for Chelsea. I hear one bloke inform another that the reason for the previous week's defeat to Barnsley stemmed from not one but two black players wearing Chelsea blue (Another youngster the

England youth international Keith Jones appeared as a late substitute).

The comment is met with mention of the fact that an unfortunate own goal by Kevin Hales hadn't helped matters.

"He's alright... he's white!" came the retort.

In the midst of this conversation, Kevin Lock nets an equaliser from a free kick some 20 yards out.

An entertaining game finishes with honours even and our performance is much better than of late.

Turning to leave, I wondered whether those who didn't want to see black players at Chelsea would continue following the club. With that notion, my thoughts turn to the youth team where there are a number of promising black players who may soon be vying for a place in the first team.

However, back to today's proceedings and I then wonder if we may have derailed Fulham's promotion bid and now look forward to Easter Monday's home game with leaders QPR.

It remains to be seen just how many west London clubs will make it to the top flight come the end of the season but for us we can only plan for the next campaign.

Rumour has it John Neal is planning further raids upon his former clubs Middlesbrough and Wrexham to provide some added steel to the side. Perhaps together with those aforementioned youngsters we will indeed see some "proper entertainment" next season.

Grimsby Town 2 Chelsea 0
13th December 1980

Football League Division Two
Blundell Park
Chelsea; Petar Borota, Gary Locke, Dennis Rofe, John Bumstead, Micky Droy, Gary Chivers, Ian Britton, Mike Fillery, Colin Lee, Clive Walker, Peter Rhoades-Brown (Phil Driver)
Manager; Geoff Hurst
Referee; Alex Hamil
Attendance; 14,708

It's Thursday night before another jaunt north and, after training for my Sunday football team, I head to The Swan for a couple of pints with Frank.

Frank is in his early 80s and has followed Chelsea all of his life. I'm always asking him about the past and of his finest moments watching the Blues.

He was there amongst a crowd estimated at 100,000 for the visit of the legendary Moscow Dynamo just after the Second World War and vehemently agrees with Tommy Lawton's observation that Bobrov's goal which tied the game at 3-3 was yards offside.

Lawton later told the assembled hacks that the referee, Lieutenant Commander G Clark (Royal Navy), had awarded the goal for 'diplomatic reasons'.

Lawton complained, "I told him that he'd done us out of our winners' bonus."

Frank bemoaned that he had not been able to obtain a match programme as the club didn't anticipate such a crowd and not enough were printed.

Oddly, whenever I crave details of the club's only Championship win in 1955, Frank always refers to another friendly against foreign opposition and the visit of the crack Hungarian side, Red Banner, to Stamford Bridge in December 1954. The match ended 2-2 and was witnessed by over 40,000.

Frank recalls that three penalties were missed but is unsure whether we missed either one or two. He thinks the culprits were John Harris or Frank Blunstone but can't be sure.

I tell him I'm off to Grimsby for the weekend and ask if he has any recollections of visiting Blundell Park.

He recounts a visit in November 1962 when, after suffering relegation in the previous campaign, Chelsea arrived there topping Division Two.

After travelling up by a coach that departed Stamford Bridge at midnight Friday, the Blues ran out 3-0 winners. He is certain that Bobby Tambling scored two and that the team included Peter Bonetti, Ken Shellito, Bert Murray, Barry Bridges and Frank 'the Tank' Upton.

I remember, as a seven year old schoolboy, that the winter of 1963 was the coldest ever and I am informed that after Chelsea defeated Luton Town 2-0 at Kenilworth Road on Boxing Day, they did not play another league game until February 9th.

In view of the conditions, Chelsea manager Tommy Docherty took his players to train and play two friendly fixtures in Malta.

Upon their return, disaster struck and amazingly the team suffered five consecutive league defeats but still occupied first position.

Promotion was finally secured after Portsmouth were trounced 7-0 on 21st May 1963 with Tambling netting four.

Chelsea finished second, just beating Sunderland to the second promotion place by a goal difference of 0.401.

Famously, it is recorded that in the game prior to Pompey, the Blues had beaten Sunderland at Roker Park 1-0 with a goal that came from the thigh of Tommy Harmer. However, Frank recalled that, "It went in off his arse!"

At closing time, Frank wishes me a good trip and I tell him that, unlike his visit, I shall be driving up the A1 at leisure on the Friday afternoon prior to the game.

I suffered some ribbing from the lads at football training as I revealed that, upon her insistence, I am taking my girlfriend to the match this weekend!

Whilst she has no interest in the beautiful game, she is curious as to the company I keep and she's looking forward to putting the faces to the names.

The lads have located a public house with bed and breakfast from the pages of the Real Ale Guide. It is the White Swan in the racing town of Market Rasen, Lincolnshire.

Upon arrival in the late afternoon, I am pleased to see my

colleagues have already safely arrived and are gathered around the fireplace in a cosy back bar.

After introducing my partner to the lads, it becomes obvious that they arrived late morning and are suitably refreshed from sampling the house fare.

I enquire of Gary as to the whereabouts of Karen, his girlfriend who was also due to accompany him on this excursion.

He announces that she is a "miserable cow" and that their relationship is probably about to be terminated.

The boys have already obtained details of the nightspots of Market Rasen, thanks to the help of two local lasses, one of whom has had the pleasure of dispensing their drinks all afternoon.

The girls announce that they shall be more than happy to chaperone my friends around town later that evening.

My girlfriend however declines their invitation to accompany the group on this sight seeing tour and mentions that after our long trek I had promised a "romantic meal".

Our genial host, Gordon Holvey, recommends a Chinese restaurant in town which sounds good and we agree that maybe we'll join up with the boys and girls later.

In the restaurant the inquisition begins...

"Why have none of your friends got girlfriends?"
"If I had not come, would you be behaving in the same way?"

Then a statement that hits me right below the belt,

"Anyway, my dad says Chelsea are rubbish and in a division below Spurs, the team he supports."

Perhaps the restaurant is having a bad time as, contrary to Gordon's recommendation, when the two special chow mein meals arrive, they look and taste similar to the Golden Wonder 'Pot Noodle' – just add boiling water.

Back at the White Swan we thank our host and retire for the evening.

However, just after midnight, we are disturbed by "Ginge" hammering on our door.

He noisily explains that he has been refused entry at the nightclub as his corduroy trousers have been deemed inappropriate for the establishment but the others have gained admission.

He has a taxi with meter running outside and requests that, as we are about of the same stature, I lend him my kecks.

I readily agree to his request much to the dismay and annoyance of my girlfriend.

On Saturday morning she has decided that rather than make the onward journey to Grimsby she will remain in Market Rasen and look around the shops.

Fleetingly, I consider making some funds available in case she espies a nice frock or pair of shoes but then, upon checking how much I had in my wallet, realise I shall need the cash for the lads' beer kitty at lunchtime and post-match.

Taking up our seats at the game as usual, I peruse our opponent's line up.

Only two names are familiar. One is Trevor Whymark, formerly of Ipswich Town and an England International. A local behind me mentions that Whymark is in great form and a bargain £80,000 signing from Vancouver Whitecaps.

The other is Mike Brolly, once of our parish, a Scottish wide man who played only half a dozen or so games towards the end of the 1972/73 season before being transferred to Bristol City.

However, the last game of that season saw him in the exalted company of the likes of Osgood, Bonetti, Harris, McCreadie and Hollins when Bobby Charlton played his last senior game for Manchester United and 44,000 packed into a three sided Stamford Bridge whilst the East Stand structure loomed large.

We do not begin well and indeed, after the hosts spurn a host of early chances, Whymark heads home and, with only seconds remaining of the first period, local hero Tony Ford adds a second.

The second half brings no consolation for our large following but just disappointment.

The local who warned me of Whymark's prowess, delights in informing our party that, despite the fact that we arrived in second place in the table, he has not seen a worse performance from a visiting side for as long as he can remember.

Towards the end of proceedings, a voice booms through the Tannoy and declares Brolly "Man of the Match".

As the final whistle blows, it becomes evident that the sniggering of some of the locals has got under Phil's skin and we suitably restrain him from effecting an introduction and shepherd him away with promises of a good night on the town.

During the evening, we discuss why former players always seem to return to haunt us.

Phil recalls another young scot, Jim McCalliog, netting the killer goal for Sheffield Wednesday against us at Villa Park in the 1966 FA Cup Semi-Final and Jimmy Greaves and Terry Venables appearing for Spurs a year later at Wembley. In fact, the list goes on late into the Grimsby night.

Indeed, we wonder if the likes of present players, for example, Clive Walker or Peter Rhoades-Brown will ever return to hurt us.

Upon returning home on Sunday afternoon, I drop my girlfriend at the end of her road as she has told her parents that she has been on a hen party with some girls from work and not on a lads' fest to the dull East Coast.

I enquire when I shall see her midweek. She's not sure.

Oh well… I'll catch up with Frank next Thursday and all will be OK.

Huddersfield Town 1 Chelsea 1
8th January 1983

FA Cup Round 3
Leeds Road
Chelsea; Steve Francis, Colin Lee, Joey Jones, Gary Chivers, Micky Droy, Colin Pates, Mike Fillery, John Bumstead, David Speedie (Clive Walker), Alan Mayes, Peter Rhoades-Brown
Scorer; Mayes 59
Manager; John Neal
Referee; Neil Midgley (Salford)
Attendance; 17,064

Having experienced a bleak Christmas period with a goalless draw at home to Fulham on Boxing Day followed by away defeats at Shrewsbury (0-2) and Leicester (0-3), we are now to journey north again for a FA Cup third round tie.

Whist we had all hoped for a more glamorous opposition, at least we have a good chance of progressing to the next round. That said, Huddersfield are presently fourth in the Third Division and are unbeaten at Leeds Road so far this season having won nine and drawn three of their home games. We languish in fifteenth place in the Second Division.

Phil is presently living in Cropston, Leicestershire, and he and Maggie kindly accommodated half a dozen of us on New Years Eve before the fruitless trek to Shropshire and then again for the drubbing at Filbert Street.

He decides that we should meet in his new local, the Bradgate Arms, then head straight up the M1 to Yorkshire. I ask him how he and the family are settling in the East Midlands and he tells me that whilst most aspects are alright, he has worries over his eldest son's future schooling.

Stuart is approaching five years of age with younger brother Christopher just two.

We took Stuart to Leicester and whilst he was keen to sing *Blue Is The Colour* all the way to the ground, the game left him – like us all – disillusioned.

Playing devil's advocate, I playfully suggest that once he starts school he may be swayed to support the local City side after all they were quite impressive against us with two goals from a youngster named Lineker and another from an Alan Smith earning them a deserved victory.

We begin to discuss today's game, our present form and cup-ties from the past.

Phil recounts his first FA Cup 3rd round tie when, in January 1964, he queued with schoolmates through the night to obtain tickets for the replay with Spurs.

When they finally approached the turnstiles one of their number reached into his pocket only to find that his money had gone. As none of his mates were able to provide the funds he required, he began wailing.

A local bobby on crowd control immediately dried the lad's eyes and thrust a ten shilling note into his hand.

Upon returning home to Walton on Thames, Phil mentioned this compassionate act to his mother who immediately pulled out her writing bureau and wrote letters to Chelsea Football Club and Fulham Police Station in an attempt to identify the officer in question and ensure he was suitably reimbursed and commended.

Mrs Norman's letter was printed in the next matchday programme but they never learned of any happy outcome.

I mention that maybe history will be kind to us as, after we last won at Huddersfield in a 3rd round tie in 1967, the team progressed all the way to the final at Wembley.

None of us present today were there to witness goals from Peter Houseman and Bobby Tambling overturn a 1-0 deficit but, when I recall that my Uncle Raymond didn't make the trip due to fears around the foot and mouth epidemic which was prevalent in the north at the time, this provokes raucous laughter around the table.

I insist that this is true and may be verified by consulting old Chelsea programmes around the time which advised supporters intending to travel to obtain suitable inoculation.

With time knocking on, I dissuade the lads from a further whip-round and recommend we head north. I jump into Phil's new company car, a yellow Ford Capri, and we all begin singing the theme tune to 'The Banana Splits', the present Saturday morning offering from the BBC for younger viewers.

Indeed, Phil remarks that perhaps watching the TV with Stuart and Christopher would be a better alternative to today's forthcoming attraction.

Taking up our seats in the Leeds Road stadium's main stand, we observe some disturbances in the opposite Cow Shed open terrace. Police soon quell the disorder and move the visiting invaders to behind the goal to our right.

The massed ranks of Londoners then begin their anthems.

To the tune of *Lord of the Dance* they bellow that *We are the famous CFC*, a lyric that unfortunately then includes a swear word.

Sitting alongside us are a young father and son sporting home colours with the lad becoming more excitable by the second.

When he questions his father as to the words of that song, he claims not to have heard it and we exchange a knowing wink.

Quite to our surprise though, the youngster replies that he heard the 'f'-word but does not understand why Chelsea are famous!

Smilingly, the father informs his son that Chelsea once beat their nemesis Leeds United to win the FA Cup long before the boy was born.

Then another question from the boy who asks, "Are Huddersfield famous?"

The proud father nudges me and replies that they are indeed as the club once won the First Division title three years in succession but adds that it was long before any of us were born!

The teams take to the sodden, frozen turf and the parent and child study the visiting line up for famous faces.

Looking out onto the pitch, the youngster is immediately taken by the Chelsea captain, Micky Droy, and asks me how tall he is.

When I reply that he stands at some six feet and four inches, he comments that he has never seen anyone that tall so he must be famous.

Sadly, as the game progresses, there is not so much entertainment on the pitch and my mind takes me back to the first time I saw Huddersfield play at Stamford Bridge in March 1971.

On that day, a flock of pigeons landed in the centre circle and declined to take flight again.

Charlie Cooke had to dribble not only around his opponents but also the birds. The press obviously had a field day when reporting the lack of action the next morning.

Whilst that game was witnessed by some 28,000 hardy souls, three days later 45,000 saw Peter Osgood return from an eight week suspension to score twice in a 4-0 win over Bruges in the Quarter-Final of the European Cup Winners' Cup.

Since my first visit in 1966, I cannot recall a more emotional night at the Bridge as the boys in blue overturned a two goal deficit suffered in the first leg.

Back to today though and, when we fail to clear a corner, a Huddersfield defender by the name of Brian Stanton bundles the ball home.

At half time, our new acquaintance now relieved of his son who is escorted to the toilets by his mother, extends New

Year's wishes to us and offers some cigars and a tot of brandy from his concealed hip flask.

Phil enjoys the Slim Panatela but remarks that we are not likely to be celebrating anything soon.

However cometh the hour cometh the man!

Alan Mayes, our recent £200,000 signing from Swindon Town, finds some space on the right hand side of the penalty area and fires home sending the travelling support of some three thousand delirious.

The youngster becomes inquisitive again and asks me as to Mayes' credentials.

I inform him that he is indeed famous as before he joined Chelsea he netted a unique treble for Swindon at nearby Rotherham.

After some delay Phil and the boy's father enquire as to Mayes' hat-trick and why I described it as "unique".

Smugly, I inform them that the first two were netted in Swindon's white away kit but at the interval the referee had deemed that there was a clash of colours and ordered that they wore Rotherham's away strip of all blue in the second period when Mayes netted his third.

After some head shaking and sighing, Phil asked if I received any other Christmas presents apart from that new anorak.

The game peters out to a draw and, leaving the ground, we thank the lad and his parents for the afternoon's entertainment and wish them well in their promotion campaign.

Journeying back down the M1, we reflect on the afternoon's fare and contemplate the forthcoming replay on Wednesday.

Phil won't be able to make it but will be down next Saturday for the visit of Cambridge United.

Switching vehicles back in Leicester for the onward trip home, I console Phil as to our team's present position and compliment him on teaching young Stuart the lyrics to *Blue Is The Colour.*

We agree that hopefully he may never join in with *Carefree* though and we bade each other goodnight with the cleaner chant of *We are the famous, the famous Chelsea* a tune adopted from a chart success *Nut Rocker* by Bee Bumble and the Stingers.

It's the draw for the fourth round at Monday lunchtime and I'll take my transistor radio to work hoping that we may land a plum tie should we overcome the three times Champions of the First Division!

Here's hoping.

Ipswich Town 2 Chelsea 0
21st September 1974

Football League Division One
Portman Road
Chelsea; John Phillips, Gary Locke, Peter Houseman, John Hollins, John Dempsey, Ron Harris, David Hay, Chris Garland, Charlie Cooke, Ian Hutchinson, John Sissons
Sub not used; Micky Droy
Manager; Dave Sexton
Booked; Hollins
Referee; Harry New
Attendance; 23,121

This is my first away game of the season having missed the 3-1 win at Coventry and the midweek 2-1 victory at Burnley.

When both of those games were being played I was in Paignton, Devon beside my transistor radio in a tent praying for victories.

Now I have returned to school to continue in the second year sixth pursuing A Levels in Mathematics, Further Mathematics and English Literature.

Today I have elected to travel by way of the football special from Liverpool Street as it is as cheap as the Chelsea Supporters' Club coach and quicker.

Upon boarding, it soon becomes apparent that not everyone will have a seat and the police officers herd youths up and down the aisle before realising that this is the case and many will stand for the hour and a half journey.

Unlike the Supporters Club excursions though, there is a distinct lack of acceptable social behaviour or etiquette nor indeed any intelligent conversation around current affairs or the beautiful game.

The youths around me spend most of their time discussing the previous Saturday when Arsenal visited the Bridge but there is no mention of John Dempsey's long awaited return from injury and his sterling performance in the goalless draw.

They speak only about the violence which had ensued when a mob of several hundred infiltrators from north London to the Shed End were identified just before kick off and repelled over the perimeter walls onto the dog track in front of the West Stand benches.

I long to have a conversation around the recent signings David Hay from Celtic, who joined for a record fee of £225,000, and the veteran former West Ham winger John Sissons, purchased for a more modest £50,000 from Norwich.

As the train slows to pass through Chelmsford the yobs pull down the carriage windows and hurl insults at anybody going about their business on the station platforms.

Some twenty minutes later, the travelling public of Colchester suffer the same fate.

We alight at Ipswich to be welcomed by the East Anglian Constabulary, complete with two mounted policeman and baying Alsatian dogs.

The youths around me are concerned that, as we are frogmarched to Portman Road, they may not have an opportunity to escape the escort and access the home terrace for their intended afternoons 'sport'.

We are channelled into the away terrace behind one of the goals and I jostle for a good vantage point to view the game and get one from above an exit.

The youths around me though only have their eyes fixed upon the home terrace at the other end of the ground and greet a public disturbance there with loud appreciative applause.

Once order is restored, the visiting miscreants are escorted to our end by the police and are welcomed into our throng with chants acclaiming them as loyal supporters.

Upon hearing the team line-ups, we learn that a youngster named Colin Viljoen, who has been receiving rave reviews from the press this season, will be wearing the number eight shirt for the hosts.

Viljoen is South African but has applied for British Citizenship and has expressed a desire to play for England. His manager, Bobby Robson, has stated that the process needs to be accelerated as he is indeed good enough to play for the national team at this time.

Manager Dave Sexton is continuing to select Peter Houseman in the Chelsea line-up at left back. This, despite the fact that he has always figured as either a winger or midfielder in his time with us featuring in the cup successes of 1970 and 1971.

The number eleven shirt vacated by Houseman will be worn by the new recruit Sissons who Sexton has admired for sometime as a quick, direct wide man.

Many eyebrows were raised as to Sissons inclusion in the subsequent defeat to Carlisle United on the opening day of the season. Sexton explained that he required the ball to be delivered quickly from the left flank for the likes of Ian Hutchinson and Chris Garland.

David Hay is wearing the seven shirt but I am unsure whether he will be in a defensive or attacking position.

Charlie Cooke is to wear the number nine shirt but even most of the hooligans assembled here know he is not going to be playing at centre forward.

I feel it is a clever ploy on Sexton's part as, for nearly ten years, the supporters' favourite, Peter Osgood, excelled wearing the number nine and in some peoples eyes nobody will ever be deemed fit enough to literally fill his boots.

Chris Garland has recently suffered verbal abuse from the terraces when wearing nine but Charlie Cooke is unlikely to receive the same treatment as, like dearly missed Ossie, he is hailed as a club legend – the Bonny Prince of Stamford Bridge.

Only three minutes into the game and Brian Talbot gives Ipswich the lead ably assisted by an astute cross-field ball from Colin Viljoen.

Going into the interval and Chelsea have yet to muster a meaningful attack and I am still unsure as to David Hay's intended position. Furthermore, Sissons is not delivering the ball quickly or indeed at all. He bears little resemblance to the man I recall scoring twice for West Ham in a classic 5-5 draw at the Bridge in December 1966.

Soon after the break and Viljoen is at it again this time providing an excellent cross for David Johnson to head home.

Whilst Charlie tries hard to get us back into the game, it is only the excellence of Chelsea goalkeeper John Phillips that keeps the score at 2-0.

Coming back on the train, I take out the paperback I am currently enjoying *Adolf Hitler – My Part In His Downfall* by Spike Milligan and try to forget about the game and the present company.

All the talk around me is not about the performances of the likes of Hay or Sissons but about possible confrontations with hooligan factions from Tottenham Hotspur or West Ham once we arrive back in London.

A thickset gentleman in his late 20s or early 30s brushes past me and guffaws at my choice of literature then accuses some of the youths around me of not showing up at Middlesbrough a couple of weeks ago when apparently he suffered a beating.

He informs them that their reputations will be redeemed in his eyes if they accompany him to Euston where the Spurs fans will be returning from their match at Wolverhampton.

They all agree that they will head over there via the Circle Line from Liverpool Street to form a welcoming party.

Arriving back, I immediately head for a newspaper stand

and purchase the Evening News to peruse the day's results.

Amazingly, whilst Spurs have won 3-2 at Molineux and West Ham have defeated Leicester 6-2 at home, Chelsea – in fourteenth place – remain London's top placed side ahead of those two clubs as well as Arsenal and QPR.

Viljoen inspired Ipswich Town are top of the First Division.

I try to avoid those heading to Euston but it is almost inevitable as I need to take the same Circle Line route to Paddington. Hopefully, they will disembark there and the rest of my journey will be stress free.

However, just one stop down at Moorgate, we experience a long delay and through the train windows it becomes evident that the tube adjacent is housing up to one hundred youths sporting the claret and blue of West Ham United.

A station operative then enters our carriage and orders everybody off as someone has pulled the emergency chord.

More worryingly though, the youths in the adjacent tube are exiting their carriages and I feel it may not be too long before they find their way over to our platform.

Those around me immediately take flight and head for adjoining exits towards the front of the train.

I look around me and note the presence of a few tourists and theatregoers and take up a bench seat amongst them.

Seconds later, the West Ham hooligans are racing past us

in pursuit of the fleeing Chelsea boys.

I take out *Adolf Hitler* again and bury my head in it whilst at the same time dexterously remove my Chelsea lapel badge and place it deep in my pocket.

Thankfully, despite some enquiring looks, the gangs continue past me and out into the streets.

Back home I retire and contemplate the day's events.

Tomorrow afternoon I am calling around to Claire's house as she is also studying English Literature.

We will be discussing amongst other worldly affairs Shakespeare's *Antony and Cleopatra* , Chaucer's *Pardoners Tale*, the verse of Thom Gunn and Ted Hughes and *Brighton Rock* by Graham Greene.

I don't think I'll recount to her my reflections on some of the behaviour that I've witnessed today and I doubt if she'll have any thoughts or opinion as to Dave Sexton's tenure as manager of Chelsea Football Club.

Goodnight.

Kilkenny 1 Chelsea 8
3 August 1986

Pre-season friendly
Buckley Park
Chelsea; Tony Godden, Darren Wood, Colin Pates, John Bumstead, Joe McLaughlin, Steve Wicks, Pat Nevin, Mickey Hazard, Kerry Dixon (Roy Wegerle), Gordon Durie, John McNaught
Referee; J Jackman
Attendance; 3,500

After yesterday's shenanigans, we are heading south from Dublin today to Kilkenny for another friendly. We have sought assurances that our opponents EMFA Kilkenny only ever play their home games at Buckley Park.

Having retired in the small hours and waking a little later than we intended, we decide to skip the full Irish breakfast. However, Mrs McDonagh waves us off with a couple of packs of bacon sandwiches (no cabbage).

Heading south we discuss the previous evening's 3-2 victory over Dundalk.

Steve Wicks, who was one of the heroes of Eddie McCreadie's 1977 promotion winning side, has now rejoined the club from QPR. Quite surprisingly manager, John Hollins, has experimented with the back four and, with Wicks returning to the centre of defence, has moved supporters' favourite, Colin Pates, to left back.

We are all a little mystified by this as Patesy has only ever played as a left sided centre back. Furthermore will this mean that another firm favourite and last night's emergency linesman, Dougie Rougvie, will be leaving?

Tony regularly watches the youth team near his home at Harlington on Saturday mornings and has followed the progress of a young Scottish left back named John Millar and reckons it won't be long before he is pressing for a place in the first team.

To while away the time as we pass the green fields, I ask the boys to name players who, like Wicks, have left the club only to return at a later date.

The first that I can recall is Allan Harris, brother of Ron our FA Cup winning captain, who returned from Coventry and appeared alongside his sibling in the 1967 FA Cup Final defeat to Tottenham.

The lads begin sniggering when I mention that I feel that Joe Kirkup and not Allan Harris should have been selected for that game and perhaps Ron had had a word in manager Tommy Docherty's ear around who was the better right back.

Before arriving in the historic city, the names of Cooke, Osgood, Hudson and present manager Hollins have all been added to the list.

We then have a further debate around whether these players' second stints at the Bridge were deemed successful or otherwise.

I think that we agree that in Charlie Cooke and John Hollins cases, as they both played their part in successful promotion winning sides, the answer is "Yes" but with

Ossie and Huddy – and as much as we loved seeing them return – it's a "No".

After a whistle stop sight seeing tour of Kilkenny, we locate Buckley Park and park up.

Strangely it reminds me of my local Windsor Great Park where the Queen attends polo matches. The ground has no perimeter walls and the pitch is protected from the public by poles with ropes.

A wooden shack appears to be the teams changing room and has a sign affixed;

EMFA Kilkenny FC – Strictly No Camping.

We enter the clubhouse and proceed to the bar and are greeted by two Dublin lads who have also travelled down by train after last night's game.

Making our introductions, we learn that Dave and Paddy-Joe are awaiting the arrival of their fellow Chelsea supporter, Derry, who is making his way over from Wexford.

Indeed, whilst we are quaffing the first of the day they espy him from the window.

Derry is alone and dismounts from a large HGV tow truck. When he enters the building he receives some ribbing from his mates as to his attire.

He is dressed in shorts, open toe sandals and knee length socks. Paddy-Joe jokes that whilst we were watching the game last night, Derry was attending a boy scouts' jamboree.

Over a couple of pints, we learn that Dave and Paddy-Joe have booked their flight over for the opening home game of the season when we are to host Norwich City and will kip down at Dave's sister's flat in Balham as she is currently working in London.

They try to get to the Bridge a couple of times a season and also to games in Liverpool and Manchester when funds and ferries permit.

Derry has never been to England and cant remember exactly how and when his love affair with the Blues began. He thinks it must have been when Chelsea played a pre-season friendly at Waterford in August 1968 and thrilled the locals when winning 5-2.

Amazingly, he is able to name the Chelsea line-up upon that day complete with substitutes and goal scorers. He then informs me that a couple of weeks later, "On the 24th", he listened on the radio as his adopted heroes trounced European Cup holders Manchester United 4-0 at Old Trafford.

Again he recites the team this time with the times of the goals.

"Tommy Baldwin after just thirty nine seconds then Tambling on thirteen minutes, Baldwin again on thirty nine and Alan Birchenall, just after the hour."

Our conversation is interrupted when an excited youngster races into the club and announces that the Chelsea team coach can be seen approaching from the foot of the hill.

We take our glasses outside and the coach pulls up to tumultuous applause from the locals. As the players begin their walk to the dressing room, I note their inquisitive looks as to the humble surroundings.

Taking up our viewing positions behind the ropes, the matchday announcer adjacent to us is experiencing some difficulty distinguishing the visiting players from the pen-pictures in the programme and the men assembled on the pitch.

At one stage, he confuses Steve Wicks with Kerry Dixon as although they play in completely different positions they both possess blonde locks.

The young lad who announced the arrival of the team coach delights in correcting his elder and then asks me the names of the Chelsea substitutes who are warming up in front of us.

He then takes out his programme and asks me how to spell "Wegerle", the surname of substitute Roy our recent acquisition from Tampa Bay Rowdies.

Much to our new friend's amusement, not only am I unsure how it is spelt, I am also unsure how it is pronounced!

I divert the conversation to the Kilkenny team line-up and the youngster quickly informs me that two sets of brothers are to play for the hosts.

I jot their names onto my team sheet; Mick and Pat Madigan and Shane and Kiernan O'Brien. Apparently, a third Madigan brother had pleaded with the Kilkenny manager to be included in this prestigious fixture but has been left disappointed.

Despite the state of the pitch and lack of facilities, the Chelsea team delight the large crowd of over three thousand with a fine display of attacking football.

At the conclusion, there is no need for me to confirm the scorers to either Derry or the youngster but, for the record, Dixon and Gordon Durie have netted trebles and further goals from Pat Nevin and Micky Hazard have given Chelsea an 8-1 win.

The largest cheer of the afternoon was reserved however for one of the O'Briens netting Kilkenny's lone strike.

Bidding farewell to our new friends in the car park before heading back to Dublin, the youngster proffers his autograph book to me and requests my signature alongside those of Chelsea players John McNaught, Joe McLaughlin and Darren Wood.

Somewhat embarrassed, I explain that I am not a club official but the lad insists that I sign "as a loyal supporter from London".

I oblige and then Derry thrusts a twenty Irish punt note into my hand together with a piece of paper with his home address written upon it.

In his soft Irish brogue, he makes an earnest request that when I attend any Chelsea away fixture in the ensuing season I post him a matchday programme and when the money is running out write to let him know and he'll send some more.

I promise to do so and also provide Dave and Paddy-Joe of the location of the Mitre Public House in Dawes Road Fulham in order that we may reciprocate their hospitality when they come over for the opening fixture of the season.

The following day before boarding the breakfast time flight from Dublin to Heathrow, I make a call to the office to assure them that whilst I am in the dentist's chair first thing, I will be back at my post by mid-morning.

Sitting back in my seat on the aircraft, I reflect on my first visit to the Emerald Isle and the kindness of Mrs McDonagh and the friendliness of our fellow supporters across the water.

Thinking ahead, I wonder if Pates at left back is going to work and whether Dougie's days with us are numbered. Will young John Millar be given his chance?

More importantly how do you pronounce "Wegerle"?

What a weekend!

Leicester City 2 Chelsea 0
15th April 1989

Football League Division Two
Filbert Street
Chelsea; Dave Beasant, Steve Clarke, Tony Dorigo, Graham Roberts, Joe McLaughlin, John Bumstead (David Lee), Kevin McAllister, Peter Nicholas, Kerry Dixon, Gordon Durie, Kevin Wilson
Unused sub; Ken Monkou
Sent off; Nicholas
Manager; Bobby Campbell
Referee; Tom Fitzharris
Attendance; 19,468

After clinching promotion back to the top flight with a 3-2 win at West Bromwich Albion last Saturday, we intend to keep the celebrations going and secure the Second Division Championship with six fixtures remaining. A points total of over one hundred is also possible – quite a contrast from the opening six games which resulted in three draws and three losses.

Indeed, the task facing the club had been made even more difficult after the Football Association ordered that the first six home games be played without any terrace admission at either end of the ground as punishment for crowd disorder at the play-off match with Middlesbrough at the end of the previous season.

The opening day fixture with Blackburn Rovers was

watched by a crowd of 8,722 and only bettered in a midweek defeat to Manchester City when an attendance of 8,858 was recorded.

A League Cup second round second leg tie with Scunthorpe United saw 5,814 hardy souls witness Chelsea's exit from the competition after a 2-2 draw gave the visitors a 6-3 aggregate win.

It was the 22nd October before the Shed was allowed to re-open and a crowd of 12,658 celebrated with a 5-0 victory over Plymouth Argyle. Since those opening six games the team have recorded 24 wins, 7 draws and suffered only one defeat, 3-0 at Hull City.

We have decided unanimously to head for the White Horse in Leire near Lutterworth as recommended by the Good Beer Guide and remembered from previous stopovers when heading south down the M1.

Whilst we are buoyantly discussing our fixture, championship prospects and even next season many of the locals are transfixed to the pub's TV and previews of the two FA Cup Semi-Finals also taking place on this day.

At Villa Park, underdogs Norwich City are playing Everton whilst further north, Liverpool and Nottingham Forest are meeting at Hillsborough, Sheffield.

Arriving at Filbert Street, we find a parking space in a nearby road and begin to make our way to the ground. A Ford transit van moves slowly past us and then the back doors open.

Three or four burly youths disembark and confront us suggesting that we are Leicester fans but before any assault occurs I convince them that we are Chelsea followers and produce enough evidence in the form of my lapel badge.

Our aggressors seem disappointed and, after three of the four re-enter their transport, the tail-ender is welcomed back aboard with an accompanying boot to his rear from my brother.

Thankfully, they continue up the road obviously hoping to make new friends along their chosen path in life.

Not long after our game kicks off, it becomes noticeable that there is some distraction from the celebratory mood beforehand. There is almost an eerie silence and murmurs can be heard from those around us.

I turn to a fellow supporter behind me who is wearing a headset and he informs me that in the FA Cup Semi-Final between Liverpool and Nottingham Forest play has been suspended due to a pitch invasion.

As half time approaches, we understand that play has still not resumed at Hillsborough and the players left the field just six minutes after kick off.

Seeking refreshment at the interval, most of the talk is around news from Sheffield and not our poor performance thus far with the game goalless.

There's an assumption that there has been an altercation on the pitch between the two sets of fans. I find this largely unlikely given the importance of the game and that the same venue hosted the very same fixture in the previous season without any apparent disorder.

Whilst Leicester score twice late in the game through Peter Reid and Nicky Cross to condemn us to only our second defeat in thirty three games, we are astonished to hear that the Liverpool versus Nottingham Forest game has been abandoned.

Returning to the car, I am about to get in when a gentleman passing by with a radio to his ear remarks, "20 dead they reckon..."

His words leave me confused but I am filled with trepidation.

Our car radio merely crackles given it's age and we head home still none the wiser as to the events which have unfolded at Hillsborough but my gut feeling is that perhaps something quite dreadful has happened.

We learned, when leaving Filbert Street, that in the other FA Cup Semi-Final, Everton had beaten Norwich 1-0 with our former favourite, Pat Nevin, scoring the only goal.

When refuelling at a service station on the way back, we come across a coach load of southern based Evertonians and I recognise a couple of them from a social gathering a year before hand when we enjoyed a quiz and darts evening at the Barbican.

I offer my congratulations to them but their jaws drop and shaking their heads they ask me if I know what has happened in Sheffield.

In hushed tones I quickly learn that the "20" is nearer to perhaps 100 people who have perished in a crush at the stadium.

I still want to believe that this is hearsay and that there will not be any fatalities once everything has been made clear.

Arriving home, I make my way up the garden path and can

see my parents watching the television and I'm still hoping for confirmation that matters are not as bad as the Evertonians have led me to believe.

However, when entering the living room, the images are being replayed on the television screen with both my mother and father viewing in stunned silence.

I begin to realise from the commentary and accounts of those interviewed that it is far worse than I ever imagined.

My mother relates to me that one gentleman is seeking news of his two daughters who were in the Leppings Lane terrace, where the casualties have occurred, whereas he had been sitting in the adjacent Cantilever stand.

She has been crying and lifts her reading glasses to wipe away some tears.

After an hour or so, I cannot continue to take in the enormity of this tragedy and make my way upstairs and lay on top of my bed and stare at the ceiling.

I am finding it hard to fathom just how so many spectators could be herded into the terrace enclosures when the match is all ticket and the numbers limited accordingly.

In the past, I have watched Chelsea play from the Leppings Lane terrace and on occasion from the seating above it. What on earth has gone wrong?

I recall my mate Ray, a Spurs fan, telling me of his experience at another FA Cup Semi-Final when his team faced Wolves at Hillsborough in 1981.

He had told me that there were too many fans admitted at the Leppings Lane End and when a crush began he and others scaled the perimeter fence to escape injury.

However, others were not so lucky and suffered leg and arm fractures.

TV pictures the following day evidenced St Johns Ambulance crews rushing to that end of the stadium and casualties being lead away upon stretchers. Spurs fans who had spilled over onto the pitch side were allowed to continue to watch whilst crouched down.

I then thought back to my own experiences.

As a fourteen year old in January 1971, I had gone with schoolmates to my first away FA Cup tie at Crystal Palace. That day, we joined in with the swaying Chelsea contingent in the Whitehorse Lane End and spent most of the afternoon trying to stay on our feet amid the massed ranks bobbing up and down.

Trailing by two goals to one and with time running out, Charlie Cooke took off on one of his mesmerising runs and provided Tommy Baldwin with a tap in for an equaliser.

In the ensuing melee on our terrace, Steve became engulfed and fell down into a sea of Doctor Martens boots. Thankfully, he was returned upright after only a few seconds by some adults around us but I remembered his ashen face when resurfacing.

Later that evening, when we changed trains at Rayners Lane on the way home, a ticket collector commented upon our blue regalia and added that we were to consider ourselves lucky that we had not been in Glasgow that afternoon.

Just like today, I was confused by this comment only to learn the following day that 66 spectators had died in a crush on stairs exiting Ibrox Park after Rangers had drawn with Celtic. A further 200 were injured.

More recently, in May 1984, I remembered Chelsea visiting Grimsby Town to play in the last game of the season when a 1-0 win secured the Second Division Championship.

Although the game was made all ticket, many of my Chelsea supporting colleagues who did not qualify for admission through either being a season ticket holder or club member, decided to make the trip on the off-chance of getting into the compact Blundell Park ground.

Indeed, when I proffered my terrace ticket at the gate, the match-day stewards appeared to be ushering everybody into the ground quickly and I heard some around me sniggering that they had not even paid to get in.

Taking up a position above an exit gate to the far left of the away terrace, I could see that, as kick off approached, there were far too many people in this end and everybody around me was uncomfortable with the situation.

Inevitably, just after the game started, Chelsea supporters began scaling the high perimeter fence and dropped below behind the goalmouth. Play was halted and two mounted policemen appeared to endeavour to restore order.

As more and more spectators poured over the barriers, the ground staff sensibly moved those affected to other parts of the ground and the Chelsea Chairman, Ken Bates, appeared on the touchline appealing for calm.

Thankfully, at the end of the afternoon, our followers were able to celebrate with the players and there were no serious injuries reported but it had been a close thing.

When an announcement came over the Tannoy that there was a crowd of some 13,000 in attendance, one of our number jokingly enquired whether that was just the visitors as, from surveying the attendance, it looked like it was probably nearer 20,000.

Today had been intended to also be one of celebration. However, I have to reflect that I believe it will be indelibly etched in my memory for the rest of my life.

It may be months or even years before the truth be known as to why so many innocent people went to support their team and did not return home to their loved ones.

There but for the grace of God.

Middlesbrough 7 Chelsea 2
16th December 1978

Football League Division One
Ayresome Park
Chelsea; Bob Iles, Graham Wilkins, David Stride, John Bumstead, Steve Wicks, Ron Harris, Ian Britton, Tommy Langley, Peter Osgood (Clive Walker 46), Trevor Aylott, Garry Stanley
Scorers; Osgood 25, Bumstead 61
Manager; Danny Blanchflower
Referee; David Clarke
Attendance; 15,107

After suffering five successive defeats, we remain bottom of the First Division.

Soon after last Saturday's 0-1 home defeat to Aston Villa, it was announced that Manager Ken Shellito had been relieved of his duties and later in the week former Northern Ireland Manager Danny Blanchflower was unveiled as our new boss.

Blanchflower captained Tottenham Hotspur when they won the double in 1961 and is renowned for his apparent wit. However, I was not amused upon seeing him interviewed upon TV after his appointment and, when asked by two young supporters whether he would keep us up, he commented, "Maybe next season!"

The much more exciting news however is that, after

months of speculation, Peter Osgood, the King of Stamford Bridge, has been signed from Philadelphia Fury for a nominal fee of £25,000.

Ossie was sold to Southampton for £275,000 in March 1974 after more than ten years in the first team after graduating through the youth ranks. When Chelsea finally secured their first FA Cup in 1970, he notably scored in every round, a feat which has never been repeated.

Furthermore, he also netted in both the European Cup Winners' Cup Final and replay the following season when the club defeated the legendary Spanish giants Real Madrid.

Frank rang me when the signing was announced and asked if I was travelling up to Middlesbrough to witness 'the second coming'.

I confirmed that indeed I was, and enquired if he had ever been there.

Laughingly he recounted how he had gone to a midweek League Cup tie at Ayresome Park in September 1967 on a coach which left Stamford Bridge on a Wednesday morning and arrived back in time for him to go straight to work the next day.

He said he had felt quite proud to be part of the smallest away contingent he could remember at an away fixture as, by his estimation at least, the Chelsea support probably numbered two hundred in a crowd of over 30,000.

As for the game, we were humbled 2-1 by the Second Division underdogs, Charlie Cooke netting a late consolation goal for us.

Frank informed me that the second Boro goal came after their left back, Geoff Butler, had raced almost the length of the pitch to provide the assist for the scorer David Smith.

Two days later, Tommy Docherty signed the young Butler for £60,000 and he debuted in a 0-3 defeat at Nottingham Forest the following Saturday.

In the next away game, Chelsea suffered a 0-7 defeat at Leeds and Docherty tendered his resignation a few days later, Geoff Butler being his last signing for the club.

Butler made only eight appearances for Chelsea and was only on the winning side once in a 3-2 win at Sunderland, a game in which Alan Birchenall marked his debut with a goal after just four minutes.

Butler obviously made an impression in that game though as it was Sunderland who took him back to the North East for a fee of £65,000.

Departing by train from Kings Cross soon after 9.00am, all the talk is around Osgood and Blanchflower. The romantics are convinced that the returning Messiah will deliver and lead us up the table but, as for the ex-Spurs man, well...

I recline in my seat and think back to my first ever game at the Bridge on Easter Saturday April 9th 1966 when I was taken to Stamford Bridge and told that I would see, amongst others, the lean skilful number 9, Osgood, strut his stuff.

Whilst on that day, Peter did not get on the score sheet, he laid on four of the six goals in a 6-2 rout of West Ham United.

Viewing from the West Stand benches, I was surprised to hear some of my elders pre-match expressing their displeasure that Osgood's inclusion 'demoted' the supporters' favourite and England International Barry Bridges to the right wing in the number 7 shirt. Afterwards however, everyone seemed happy.

The following season, I witnessed perhaps the finest solo effort ever seen at the Bridge when, at the start of the second half in a game with Southampton and trailing 0-3, Ossie weaved his way through as many as six opponents before side stepping the keeper and netting at the Shed End. Alas, the game ended in a 2-6 reverse, but that strike would never be forgotten.

One of my best memories of nights at the Bridge goes back to March 1971 and the European Cup Winners' Cup Quarter-Final with Bruges.

After suffering a 0-2 defeat in Belgium, Chelsea recorded a magnificent 4-0 win to progress to the Semi-Finals.

Peter Osgood returned to the side that night after serving a six match suspension imposed by the Football Association under their 'totting up' rules after he had picked up a number of bookings.

With Chelsea leading 1-0 from a Peter Houseman effort and with time running out, Ossie netted in front of the North Stand and immediately hurdled the advertising hoardings pursued by photographers, peanut sellers and ball boys!

In extra-time, he netted again at the Shed End after a superb mazy dribble and cutback from the byeline by the immaculate Alan Hudson. With the crowd still celebrating Tommy Baldwin added the fourth, sending the whole ground into delirium.

I have never witnessed a better atmosphere than on that night at Stamford Bridge.

After arriving at Ayresome Park, the four of us purchase stand seats and enquire at the box office window as to the proximity of a suitable hostelry for lunch.

Worryingly, the lady behind the counter advises us to take care as visiting supporters are rarely tolerated by the locals!

Whilst heeding her advice, we head around to a social club in the adjacent stand but when queuing to go in, hear a commotion inside the building and the sound of breaking glass.

We are then turned away by the doorman and witness Michael Greenaway and his entourage being ejected.

We make do with hot pies and coffees in the stand on what must be the coldest day of the year.

The Chelsea team is announced and Peter Osgood will wear the number 9 shirt exactly 14 years to the day he debuted for the club when scoring twice in a 2-0 win at Workington in a League Cup tie.

Ossie is now 31 years old, whereas Tommy Langley wearing number 8 is 20 and number 10 Trevor Aylott is 21.

Indeed, the team is a mixture of youth and experience with full backs Graham Wilkins and David Stride and midfielder John Bumstead also in their early 20s and FA Cup winning captain Ron Harris is aged 34.

With the game scoreless and nearly half an hour played, the Messiah does not disappoint, Ossie rising majestically to head home.

In view of the pre-match warning received from the lady in the ticket office, our celebrations are somewhat muted but enough to turn many heads in the rows of home fans in front of us.

However, before half time, Middlesbrough net three goals and we are no longer the centre of attention.

When the teams re-emerge after the break, we notice that substitute Clive Walker, another youngster, has replaced Osgood.

Things become even worse when Boro soon score a fourth before Chelsea pull one back with a goal fashioned in East London. Bermondsey born Aylott's header is blocked on the line but Bumstead from Rotherhithe forces the ball home.

Normal service though is quickly resumed and, before final whistle, the home side hit another three to give them a 7-2 victory. Amidst all the action, I am unsure just how many goals have been scored by Tommy Burns but I think it is probably four.

Seconds before the end, a match steward approaches us and suggests that his team escort us away to the exit as he feels we may still be a target for abuse from the celebrating locals.

Leaving the ground, we head down the high street towards the railway station in advance of the Chelsea contingent who are accompanied by a police escort. However, as we go, we receive a number of verbal threats from local youths and keep on our toes.

Ginger then decides that he wishes to drop into Woolworths to purchase some confectionery for the trip home. Upon entering, we see Ross, a known Chelsea face who stands at some 6 feet 7 inches being pursued by several Boro hooligans.

After sidestepping them, our man ends up in the 'pick and mix' section before we decide to hotfoot it to the station.

Quite surreally, the in-store piped music is playing Christmas carols. Peace on Earth.

Upon boarding our train, we head for the buffet car where some members of the Chelsea Supporters Club are endeavouring to make light of our afternoon's thrashing by imbibing whatever is available and singing loudly,

> *The Shed looked up,*
> *And they saw a star,*
> *Scoring goals past Pat Jennings,*
> *From near and from far,*
> *And Chelsea won,*
> *As we all knew they would,*
> *'Cos the star of that great team,*
> *Was Peter Osgood,*
> *Osgood, Osgood, Osgood, Osgood,*
> *Born is the King of Stamford Bridge.*

We then learn that in the draw for the 3rd round of the FA Cup we will travel to Old Trafford to play holders Manchester United.

However, more importantly, next Saturday we entertain Bristol City before a Boxing Day trip to Southampton followed by an away fixture with Ipswich Town.

We desperately need to get some points soon or, come Easter, we will be looking at relegation back to the Second Division after only two seasons back.

Hopefully, Peter Osgood will be able to impart some of his know how and skills to the likes of Aylott, Langley and Walker and all will be okay.

Merry Christmas and a Happy New Year.

Newcastle United 0 Chelsea 0
4th April 1994

Premier League
St James' Park
Chelsea; Dmitri Kharine, Erland Johnsen, Frank Sinclair, John Spencer, Tony Cascarino, Dennis Wise, Steve Clarke, Mal Donaghy, Nigel Spackman, Craig Burley (Darren Barnard 90), Jakob Kjeldbjerg
Booked; Sinclair, Burley
Subs Not Used; Kevin Hitchcock, David Lee
Manager; Glenn Hoddle
Referee; Steve Lodge
Attendance; 32,216

I have been to every game so far this season, and hope to attend all the remaining fixtures as I have done in several other campaigns since first achieving this goal in 1984/85.

Attending today's game has proved more difficult though, as with St James' Park undergoing redevelopment, Newcastle have not made any allocations available to visiting clubs.

I knew of this early in the season and made some enquiries. Whilst the larger percentage of their support is made up of season ticket holders, each Monday before a home fixture 750 tickets are made available to the general public but they must produce evidence, in the form of a used ticket or voucher from a programme of their attendance at a previous game.

I am in the habit of visiting the Sportspages retail outlet in Charing Cross Road and the Newcastle fanzine 'Half Mag Half Biscuit' is a particularly good and interesting read.

In recent weeks, their co-authors – Reuven Fletcher and Dave Jameson – have bemoaned the lack of atmosphere at home matches without opposing fans being present and have questioned the club over their policy.

Reuven's contact details are in the fanzine so I phoned him a few weeks ago initially to compliment their publication and to explore any possibility of obtaining a ticket for our game.

After listening for several minutes as to the reasons behind Newcastle's fall from top position to third place since the turn of the year, I learn that Reuven also does not miss many of his club's matches.

I then inform him that, as Stamford Bridge is to undergo various redevelopments at the end of the season, there is every likelihood that, in accord with Newcastle's present policy, Chelsea may not accommodate visiting supporters next season – even though I have not learned of anything of the sort...

Reuven was uncomfortable with this news but I was quick to reassure him that as I had access to a number of season tickets I could guarantee him a ticket upon the condition that he could obtain one for me at St James' Park on Easter Monday.

He then informed me that Ross Fraser, editor of the Chelsea Independent fanzine, had already contacted him with a similar request and that he had secured twelve tickets.

Thankfully, I had made Ross's acquaintance a year or so ago and was able to call him immediately and receive the news that I could have one.

Despite the lack of a ticket allocation, Ron Hockings had still booked twenty reserved seats upon a Great North Eastern Railway express train for the game. Travelling up on the day from Kings Cross were a lot of familiar faces and most had obtained match tickets from the Chelsea playing staff.

Neil Barnett, editor of the Chelsea official monthly publication *Onside* interviewed a number of supporters onboard for stories as to the lengths they had gone to access the game but most did not wish to reveal their sources, although Kim and Sarah let it be known that they had complimentary tickets from Steve Clarke.

When the train stopped at York, we were amazed to see former Chelsea legend and now Brentford manager David Webb pacing the platform and peering into the carriage windows!

Taking our opportunity we informed him we were Chelsea followers and thanked him for scoring the winning goal in the FA Cup Final replay 24 years ago.

He then confessed that he was looking for one of his players who had missed their train but would not provide any further incriminating details.

Arriving in Newcastle, we meet up with Reuven and Dave in the railway buffet bar away from prying eyes of the local constabulary who thankfully appear thin on the ground.

With the financials sorted and tickets allocated, we decide to make our way to the Trent House pub adjacent to the halls of residence at Newcastle University.

On the way, we pass the Newcastle stronghold 'The Strawberry Inn' and I think back to the events which unfolded in March 1984 when it was infiltrated by Chelsea hooligans and resulted in a number of serious injuries. After a full police investigation, several arrests were made by the Tyneside constabulary at our next away game in Cardiff.

Eerily as I walk past the Metro station, I remember my first ever trip to Newcastle in September 1979 when I witnessed a Newcastle hooligan welcoming our travelling support whilst whirling a garden spade above his head. He was suitably apprehended before any injuries were incurred.

Thankfully, the atmosphere today is very relaxed mainly as there are officially no visiting Chelsea supporters.

The Trent House is filled with home fans, apart from the dozen or so of us, and has walls filled with pop music memorabilia, the majority of which featured Ska with many other artefacts from the 1960s and 1970s. It's my kind of place and our new friends are excellent hosts and company.

With kick-off approaching, we thank Reuven and Dave for their kindness and hospitality and make our way to the Gallowgate End of the Newcastle stadium.

Upon gaining access, we have decided to split up and not draw attention to ourselves but to regroup near the corner exit at 4.30.

The atmosphere is indeed somewhat muted, unlike in 1984 when 5,000 Chelsea supporters rammed the Leazes away terrace and exploded into a cacophony of noise when David Speedie put us one nil up on our way to winning the Second Division Championship.

Conversely, I also recall on my first visit in 1979 I had watched the game from the paddock in front of the main stand with Geordie relatives of my mate Steve and nearly swallowed my tongue when Mike Fillery silenced the Gallowgate End with a diving header. However, two headers from Peter Withe rescued the game for Newcastle and we sheepishly beat our retreat at the end sidestepping the baying home support.

When half time comes, there has been very little to report on with the game goalless.

Nearby, I catch sight of Tim Whittick, another Chelsea die-hard from the Supporters Club who I met back in the early 80s when backpacking around the Greek Islands of the Aegean. We exchange knowing smiles but don't dare to speak.

Then, a couple of lads next to me enquire if I heard the pre-match announcements and the names of the Newcastle substitutes.

After I attempt a north-east accent and announce that one of the substitutes is Alex Mathie the boys stifle a laugh and ask where I am from.

When I reply, "London," I receive a pat on the back and am complimented on travelling so far to support their team. In the course of conversation I hear them wrongly assume that I obviously have Geordie roots and follow Newcastle with the London Mags Supporters Group.

With the game nearing a stalemate conclusion, Ross

Fraser, Mark Pulver, Nick Brown and several others make their way over to the exit just as John Spencer wins a corner in front of us.

As Dennis Wise approaches to take the kick, he recognises all six feet seven inches of Ross and offers somewhat astonished applause and looks to have blown our cover!

When the kick is cleared, the final whistle is blown and Dennis turns again to salute probably the smallest Chelsea following on record.

The local constabulary are bemused by our presence and wrongly assume that the stewards allowed us to enter when the exits were opened near the end of the game.

After some discussion, we endeavour to break free from any planned police escort and head off back to Central Station.

In the bar on the station, we regroup and probably number 20 or so. Everybody has their own tale to tell of their day's experience.

Stan tells me that his mate Mick Nile had arranged to meet our Danish international Jakob Kjeldbjerg when the team coach arrived as he had promised to provide him with a complimentary ticket. However, when he made his way towards the bus, he was apprehended by the police and arrested!

Stan had advised Mick not to wear a Chelsea shirt but he would have none of it and has now paid the price. Will be interested to hear how Mick gets on and the nature of the charge.

As the beers begin to flow, the assembled throng cannot

resist belting out a few Chelsea anthems as they had not been able to during the afternoon.

However, this alerts the local constabulary who enter the bar and begin threatening further arrests.

Gerry Bowell is a colleague of mine at National Westminster and registered blind but never misses a game anywhere and is sitting with his guide dog and friends Breda and Joan.

As the policemen brush by, Gerry is very much aware of the situation and tells me that he could identify the presence of the officers by the smell of their rain sodden uniforms.

The police officer in charge then announces that all Chelsea followers must depart on the 5.15 train regardless of any other arrangements in place. However this seems to suit everyone.

Travelling back to London, the conversations turn from today's events onto the coming Saturday and our FA Cup Semi-Final tie with Luton Town at Wembley.

At Christmas, we had been bottom of the Premier League with relegation already looking a strong possibility.

However, the New Year saw an upturn in form and fortune with new signing Mark Stein scoring in seven consecutive games and propelling us up to 14th position where we sit today.

Furthermore, we have beaten Barnet, Sheffield Wednesday, Oxford United and Wolves and reach the last four of the FA Cup for the first time since winning the trophy in 1970.

However 'Steino' has missed the last few games through injury and his replacement, the veteran Eire International Tony Cascarino, has not found the net in his absence.

More worryingly, despite Luton being in the Second Division their forward line is lead by former Chelsea legend Kerry Dixon.

We all hope that Kerry will perform like Cascarino and not break our hearts next week.

Alighting after we arrive back at Kings Cross, we make our way along the platform to the strains of *The Blue Flag*.

> *Flying high up in the sky,*
> *We'll keep the blue flag flying high,*
> *From Stamford Bridge to Wembley,*
> *We'll keep the blue flag flying high!*

Let's hope we are able to keep this ditty going and it's not just going to be a one-off.

Come on Chelsea!

Oxford Utd 4 Chelsea 4
19th March 1988

Football League Division Two
Manor Ground
Chelsea; Perry Digweed, Steve Clarke, Tony Dorigo, Colin Pates, Steve Wicks, Darren Wood, Pat Nevin, Michael Hazard (Gareth Hall 80), Kerry Dixon, Kevin Wilson (Clive Wilson 85), John Bumstead
Scorers; Nevin 17, Bumstead 27, Dixon 44, Dixon 86
Manager; Bobby Campbell
Referee; Neil Midgley
Attendance; 8,468

Today we are visiting Oxford United who presently are bottom of the First Division and without a manager.

More worryingly though, Chelsea occupy 17th position without a league victory for seventeen games since beating today's opponents 2-1 at Stamford Bridge on the 31st October last year.

Furthermore, the top division is to be reduced to 20 teams at the end of the season with the bottom three automatically being relegated and the team finishing 18th will endure a two legged play-off against the team finishing third in the Second Division and then, if successful, the second placed side, again on a home and away basis.

Last season saw the First Division reduced to 21 teams with the three relegated clubs being Leicester City,

Manchester City and Aston Villa.

The season had begun fairly well and it's hard to fathom now that after nine league games a 3-0 victory at Watford saw us move to second in the table.

Some observers have noted that the downturn in form and fortune stems largely from the absence of Welsh International goalkeeper Eddie Niedzwiecki who left the field injured eight minutes from the end of that last win over Oxford.

Eddie's place has been taken by another Welshman, 19 year old Roger Freestone, a £95,000 signing from Newport County.

Roger has had an indifferent time between the posts but to his credit made two penalty saves in FA Cup games. Firstly in a 3rd round 3-1 win at Derby County and then early on in our 4th round exit at Manchester United when ten thousand travelling supporters saw us go down 0-2.

Chelsea have now recruited a more experienced goalkeeper in Perry Digweed, a 29 year old, on loan from Brighton having previously served Fulham and someone who is a Chelsea supporter having regularly watched from the Shed End.

Perry is playing his third game for Chelsea today having kept a clean sheet in a 0-0 home draw with Everton last week after previously conceding three on his debut at Coventry where again the game was drawn.

Taking up our position on the away terrace at the Cuckoo Lane End, I glance over at the Chelsea supporters in the seats to our left and remember that in 1985 I had thought myself lucky to have obtained a seat there, only to have a view akin to watching your television through a fireguard.

I had even attempted to climb over the fence to get into the terraces but was apprehended by a steward and a policeman. Later that season, I read that a Portsmouth fan had taken legal action against Oxford as he had an obstructed view and sought a claim under the Trade Description Act. I never heard how he got on though.

In the Oxford line up is former Chelsea player Peter Rhoades-Brown.

"Rosie" is the only Chelsea player that I can claim to know socially as a school friend of mine effected an introduction a few years ago having played in the same youth team.

After scoring in a memorable 2-0 5th round FA Cup defeat of European Champions Liverpool in 1982 and then being part of the squad that achieved promotion back to the top flight in 1984, Peter moved to Oxford when the team had a surfeit of wide players such as Pat Nevin, Clive Walker, Paul Canoville and Mickey Thomas.

I spoke with him a few weeks ago and he was quick to remind me that he usually plays well against us and indeed scored in both their wins in the 1985/86 season when they trounced us 4-1 at the Bridge and 2-1 at the Manor Ground.

Peter told me that after Oxford won the League Cup in 1986, the following week he and a few of his team mates decided to visit their local night-spot.

He was amazed when first their cab driver would not accept payment and then the club doormen ushered them through the entrance.

"You've done the city proud!" they proclaimed.

However, on their last visit and with their team occupying the bottom position, they were greeted with, "Back of the queue lads…"

Approaching half time and it finally looks as if we are going to win a game with goals from Pat Nevin, John Bumstead and Kerry Dixon giving us a 3-0 lead.

Soon after the break though, Rosie is at it again scoring their first and then laying on goals for Dean Saunders and Martin Foyle.

With less than ten minutes remaining, Kerry gets his second and looks to have secured a long overdue victory. Nevertheless, in a frantic last few minutes Saunders equalises and then has another effort ruled out for an infringement. Just before the final whistle Oxford then hit the underside of the crossbar.

18 games without a win!

There are eight league games remaining but thankfully six are home fixtures and the away games are in London at Wimbledon and West Ham.

Hopefully, by the time we entertain Charlton on the last day of the season. we shall be safe from the fear of relegation.

Sadly, we have learned today that Eddie Niedwiecki's injury is serious enough to perhaps terminate his playing career. He as become a firm favourite of the Chelsea supporters after joining from Wrexham in 1983 and being part of the great team assembled by John Neal which now appears to be disintegrating before us.

WHERE WERE YOU WHEN WE WERE SHOCKING?

Rumour has it that the club are lining up yet another goalkeeper in Kevin Hitchcock from Mansfield who suitably impressed when playing against us in the League Cup.

Southampton at home next and surely the chance to get three points?

Can't wait for this terrible season to finish and certainly do not want to witness us taking part in the bizarre play-off system now implemented.

I will ring Rosie next week and congratulate him on his fine performance today through gritted teeth!

Preston North End 1 Chelsea 0
28th February 1981

Football League Division Two
Deepdale
Chelsea; Petar Borota, Gary Locke, Dennis Rofe, John Bumstead, Micky Droy, Gary Chivers, Ian Britton, Mike Fillery, Peter Rhoades-Brown, Clive Walker, Colin Pates (Chris Hutchings)
Booked; Locke
Manager; Geoff Hurst
Referee; DA Webb
Attendance; 8,129

This is my first ever visit to Deepdale.

Earlier in the week I spoke to Frank to see if he had any recollection of games with Preston and learned that, in the 1959/60 season, Chelsea recorded a 5-4 away victory with all five goals coming from Jimmy Greaves who was 19 years of age at the time.

On the opening day of that season, Chelsea and Preston played out a 4-4 draw at Stamford Bridge with Greaves netting a hat trick. The Blues had been leading 4-1 with twenty minutes remaining.

The following season, Jimmy played his last game for Chelsea before joining A C Milan and signed off by scoring all four goals against Nottingham Forest in a 4-3 win at the Bridge.

WHERE WERE YOU WHEN WE WERE SHOCKING?

If ever Chelsea were in need of a goal scorer it is now. It is hard to believe that after a 1-1 draw at Notts County on the last day of November, when a late header from John Bumstead rescued a point, we have failed to score in nine of eleven fixtures. Indeed, we have not scored in the last five away games.

Two weeks ago we suffered a crushing 0-4 defeat at West Ham and fell from third to seventh place in the table. Back in November we had been second behind the east Londoners and scoring freely notably in a 6-0 thrashing of Newcastle United at home and in a 4-0 away win at Wrexham.

Last Saturday after a dismal 0-1 home defeat to Watford, I bought my rail ticket for today in the Chelsea Supporters Club shop at 547 Fulham Road. Whilst there, I chatted with former travel officer, Malcolm Roberts, who recalled that when Chelsea travelled to Preston for a 4th round FA Cup tie in 1969 the club, chartered a record twenty eight coaches for the game.

Whilst most supporters paid upfront, a great many only put down a deposit and then failed to make up the difference when travelling on the day. Several of the coaches were also vandalised and thereafter it was decided that only members would be able to travel to away games in the future.

Despite an appeal in the official Chelsea programme, few of the miscreants came forward to repay their debt to the club.

Arriving in Preston ahead of the Official Chelsea Supporters Club excursion, we venture out into the street. Strangely there appears to be little police presence.

Not knowing the town or location of Deepdale, we seek directions and wonder whether we should take a cab ride.

At this point, we hear a commotion some 25 yards in front of us and a group of Chelsea supporters race past us back into the railway terminus. Frighteningly one youth is bleeding from a slash to his neck.

Now the police appear and we too venture back into the station. After some discussion we decide that for once perhaps it will be wiser to await the arrival of the football special and join the police escort to the ground.

Some ten minutes later the special arrives and we are frogmarched to the ground but break off to take our places in the main stand.

When the teams are announced we hear that neither Colin Lee or Alan Mayes are playing leaving only Clive Walker as a recognised front man.

Furthermore I cannot place any of the Preston players at all but seeing their manager, Nobby Stiles, greeting Geoff Hurst before the kick-off, brings back memories of England's finest moment when they were World Champions in 1966 and the reason so many of us fell in love with the beautiful game.

As in previous weeks, the game is poor. Preston are third from the bottom and facing the prospect of dropping into the Third Division. However, on the stroke of half time, Mike Fillery endeavours to prevent a corner to the home side only to divert the ball to Preston substitute Alex Bruce to fire home.

During the interval break, I am approached by a home fan who wishes to wager ten pounds that Preston will win the match. I tell him that I am not a betting man and anyway my hunch is that they probably will anyway.

Having made my acquaintance, the gentleman then mentions that he and his wife, who is sat beside him, are shortly to motor south before flying out to join a Caribbean cruise.

He then asks if Gatwick Airport is clearly signposted from the M1. When I inform him that it is situated some thirty miles south of London towards Brighton and the south coast they appear somewhat disturbed and then spend the next twenty minutes or so arguing about their planned itinerary paying absolutely no attention to events on the playing field.

Well before the end, they depart still arguing however they miss little as Chelsea push both Micky Droy and Colin Pates forward in search of an equaliser that fails to materialise.

Just before the final whistle, a Tannoy message requests that Mrs Breda Lee of Chelsea Football Club make her way to Preston's main office.

Everybody knows Breda as a committee member of the Official Supporters Club who travels to all away games upon the chartered excursions. She is known for all her help in the 'Save the Bridge' campaign organising and collecting raffle monies on the trains and also looking after the club mascots at the home matches.

My immediate concern is that perhaps our excursion home has been cancelled for some reason.

Arriving safely back at the station, we have some time to kill before our seven o'clock departure so decide to sample the local fare of black pudding, mushy peas, chips and curry sauce washed down with two pints of Boddingtons.

Taking up our seats, I see from the carriage window Breda with her fellow stewards boarding the train accompanied by two lady police officers.

Half an hour into the return journey, I venture down to the buffet car passing the club officials and note that Breda is very upset.

In the buffet car Sean, who has been following Chelsea a lot longer than myself, informs me that Breda's son Gary has suffered a fatal fall on his way to the game from the station prior to the game.

We are all shocked by this tragic news. Gary was only 23 years of age.

Also, rumour has it he and others were fleeing some aggressors when he fell some 20 feet onto a main road.

Imparting the news to my three travelling colleagues, it is a most sombre journey back to London.

The fact that Chelsea remain seventh in the table tonight with ten matches remaining really pales into insignificance compared to a mother's loss.

R I P, Gary – you will be sadly missed.

Queen's Park Rangers 1 Chelsea 0
15th January 1974

FA Cup 3rd round replay
Loftus Road
Chelsea; John Phillips, Gary Locke, Ron Harris, John Hollins, Micky Droy, Marvin Hinton, Ian Britton, Steve Kember, David Webb, Tommy Baldwin, Michael Brolly
Sub Not Used; Garry Stanley
Booked; Harris
Manager; Dave Sexton
Referee; David W Smith
Attendance; 28,573

The bad news is that one of my idols, Alan Hudson, was sold yesterday to Stoke City for a club record fee of £240,000.

Alan had not played for Chelsea since a 0-1 home defeat to Liverpool on December 29th after another fall out with manager Dave Sexton.

Worryingly, it seems that Peter Osgood who also has not appeared since that Liverpool game is also likely to be sold to either Derby County or Southampton.

With the club struggling in the league, currently lying 18th and saddled with debts arising from the redevelopment of the East Stand, we are led to believe that there is unlikely to be any monies made available from the sales of Osgood and Hudson to fund player purchases.

As we are in the midst of the miners' strike and the 'three day week', today's 3rd round FA Cup replay has a kick-off time of 1.30 pm as floodlights cannot be used.

I have never truanted from school before but I am in a rebellious mood following Hudson's departure and feel that I need to get to the game.

After attending the assembly at Langley Grammar School, I left via the fire exit and walked to the railway station. There, I obtained a ticket before catching a Paddington bound train, changing at Ealing Broadway and alighting at Shepherds Bush on the Central Line.

As usual in this fixture, Chelsea's following outnumbers the home support and I take my red, white and green college scarf from my bag and tie it around my neck.

I bought the scarf last season before attending our 5th round FA Cup tie at Sheffield Wednesday when Peter Osgood netted the winner with a diving header, not too unlike the one in the 1970 Final replay when we won the trophy for the only time in our history.

On the way to that success, Chelsea beat QPR 4-2 at Loftus Road with Ossie netting a hat trick and David Webb scoring with an audacious volley to open the scoring after only seven minutes.

The two club's fortunes have since moved in opposite directions, with Rangers regularly occupying a top three place this season with many of their players including Parkes, Clement, Gillard, Thomas, Francis and Bowles being touted for England.

Indeed, when the teams are announced, I find it hard to believe that only four years before we boasted a side full of ball playing internationals but today we are also shorn of Bill Garner and Chris Garland through injuries so David Webb will play at centre forward with virtually unknown youngsters Ian Britton and Mike Brolly on the flanks.

The veteran defender Marvin Hinton occupies Webb's normal position at centre half alongside Micky Droy.

Rangers start on the front foot and have an early effort ruled out for an infringement and we go in at half time scoreless with Chelsea not registering an effort on goal.

A quick glance at the match programme reveals that Chelsea last exited the FA Cup at the 3rd round stage in 1962 when beaten 4-3 at Liverpool. More ominously however, they finished bottom of the First Division that season and were relegated.

Of the victorious FA Cup winning team from 1970, today only John Hollins, Ron Harris, David Webb and Tommy Baldwin feature. Indeed, Baldwin has been absent through injury for most of the season.

In the previous drawn tie, Chelsea were grateful to goalkeeper John Phillips who saved a penalty from Gerry Francis to earn the replay and today again it is his heroics that have prevented Rangers from having an interval lead.

On the terraces, along with the customary skirmishes, the Chelsea followers are split in their opinions as to whether Dave Sexton should be backed or sacked and, if he is sacked, will Osgood be reinstated and not sold.

Just after the hour mark, QPR finally find a way past Phillips with Stan Bowles netting after Chelsea fail to clear a corner from Dave Thomas.

With time running out, there appears more likelihood of the hosts extending their lead and little promise of an equaliser. The massed ranks of Chelsea supporters at both the home Loft and the away School End are both growing restless and are surging forward towards the pitch keeping the police well occupied fearing an inevitable invasion at any time.

In injury time, a final throw of the dice sees Ian Britton cross from the right at the School End and David Webb volleys against the underside of the bar and as the ball is hacked clear the whistle sounds for the end of the tie.

As the players leave the pitch, a wall collapses under the pressure of the baying Chelsea followers at the School End and the police and St Johns Ambulance volunteers rush to treat those injured.

QPR captain and former Chelsea player Terry Venables delights in victory but soon beats a hasty retreat down the players tunnel as disgruntled visiting supporters swarm onto the pitch in a mass protest.

Along with full backs Dave Clement and Ian Gillard, Venables was in the QPR team soundly beaten in the 6th round tie at Loftus Road four years previously so for him revenge is sweet.

Heading back to Shepherds Bush, I now begin to realise that it is around the time that I would normally finish school and worry if my truancy will be detected and my parents informed.

Thankfully, as today is Tuesday, I very much doubt that my absence from the two hour afternoon art session will be noticed as it is usually disruptive mayhem.

Had the game taken place on the Wednesday, I would have missed the games session, that being an eleven-a-side football match between the 'probables' and the 'possibles' at U15 level.

My absence, I believe, would have been noted by Ron Davies, the games master as, at U13 level two years earlier, he banished me to the 'possibles' after I feigned injury so as not to miss Chelsea's legendary midweek victory over Bruges in the European Cup Winners' Cup Quarter-Final.

Returning home at around the same time that I would have if I had attended school, my mother has set the dinner table and my father soon comes in from work.

He asks if I know of the result of the game and, unconvincingly, I reply "No…"

When he tells me that Chelsea have lost 1-0, I try to look dejected and surprised.

As we eat dinner, Mum enquires how school went, and when I begin to flounder with a response, Dad grins but does not comment.

With the table cleared and Mum out of the room, Dad turns to me and warns me not to ever truant again!

He then produces a copy of the Evening Standard that mentions that another of my idols, namely Charlie Cooke, is to return to Chelsea from Crystal Palace.

Perhaps all is not lost and Ossie will also decide not to pursue a move from Stamford Bridge.

Hopefully tomorrow I will impress Davies enough to ensure I play for the U15s in the game against the Licensed

Victuallers School on Saturday morning before heading up to the Bridge to witness the return of Charlie Cooke, the Bonnie Prince, against Derby County.

No homework tonight!

Rotherham United 6 Chelsea 0
31st October 1981

Football League Division Two
Millmoor
Chelsea; Petar Borota, Gary Chivers, Chris Hutchings, Colin Viljoen, Micky Droy, Colin Pates, Peter Rhoades-Brown (Alan Mayes), John Bumstead, Colin Lee, Clive Walker, Mike Fillery
Manager; John Neal
Referee; PJ Richardson
Attendance; 10,145

We've had an indifferent start to this season, presently occupying 11th position after 11 league games having won five, drawn two and suffering four defeats.

However, our spirits were lifted in midweek when, in the second leg of our League Cup tie with First Division Southampton, we triumphed 3-2 on aggregate with a 2-1 extra time win after drawing 1-1 at the Dell in the first leg.

It was fitting that Mike Fillery should head the winner after scoring the equaliser in that first leg and putting in a performance that I felt overshadowed those of the England Internationals Dave Watson, Kevin Keegan, Mike Channon and Alan Ball, all of whom appeared in the Saints' side.

We drew further satisfaction in that, due to injuries to both Petar Borota and Bob Iles, seventeen year old Steve

Francis was blooded for his debut and gave a performance which belied his age and inexperience.

So, despite last Saturday's home defeat to Barnsley, we head up the M1 buoyed by our midweek giant killing.

Over the years, we have got to know many true blue followers who live in other parts of the country and today we drop off in Chesterfield to meet up with a few who live in the vicinity.

In the Market Tavern, we continue to celebrate the team's progression to the next round of the League Cup with locals Chris Tyrell, Richard Steele, Steve Flood and Kevin and Beverly Barnes.

Kev and Bev inform us that they are to form the Chelsea East Midlands Supporters' Club and will provide transport to both home and away games for exiled Chelsea supporters in the area as well as monthly social events.

It's this type of camaraderie that keeps us going as we continue to believe we will return to the top flight some ten years after the FA and European Cup successes which many of us were lucky enough to witness.

Soon, we are back on the motorway and heading for previously unchartered territory of Rotherham.

Taking up our seats in the ground, I note from the official programme that Chelsea have only ever played one other league game at Millmoor, that being on the opening day of the 1962/63 season.

The omens would appear good however, as Chelsea recorded a 1-0 win courtesy of a goal from Bobby Tambling in a game where Eddie McCreadie made his

Blues debut and, at the end of that season, we returned to the First Division as runners-up behind Stoke City.

When the teams are announced, we learn that Yugoslavian International keeper Borota is fit and retains his position ahead of young Francis.

As usual, there is an impressive turn out from London as well as from our exiles, with some 3000 visitors swelling the crowd to over 10,000.

With only eight minutes played, the hosts take the lead through fullback Brecklin and whilst we are still allowing latecomers to find their seats around us, Rotherham net through Fern and a Moore penalty. Unbelievably, we are three down with only 13 minutes on the clock!

Petar Borota is already having a game to forget. When Fern netted the second, he took his eye off the ball and appeared to be instructing his defenders as to where he would be delivering the ball once he had it. Pure calamity!

At least when half time comes, Rotherham have not added to their lead. However, Chelsea have not tested their goalkeeper once.

In the bar at half time, we encounter former Northern Ireland international centre forward Derek Dougan, who is a co-commentator for Yorkshire TV covering the game.

I ask him if he still bears the scars from his days when playing against Ron Harris and David Webb and he smiles and then grimaces at the memories.

He then enquires as to the nationality of Borota and when we inform him that he is a Yugoslav. He laughs and comments that he should be in Disneyland.

Whilst quaffing a quick pint, Bill and I discuss the likelihood or otherwise of a famous Chelsea comeback.

Bill was at Blackpool in October 1970 when another young goalkeeper, John Phillips, debuted for the injured Peter Bonetti. Like today Chelsea trailed 0-3 at the interval but after Charlie Cooke substituted for Tommy Baldwin, he laid on two goals for Keith Weller and another for emergency striker Webb before hapless defender Dave Hatton turned in his cross for the winner giving the Londoners a 4-3 victory.

Bill recalled that, after the game, the two Chelsea Supporters Club coaches were about to depart for the Blackpool illuminations when the then manager Dave Sexton appeared and brought the players onboard to thank those who'd travelled for their vocal backing.

We were also both present at Stamford Bridge in October 1978 when, in the tenth game of the season and without a home win, Chelsea trailed 0-3 to Bolton Wanderers.

Sitting in the East Stand, we had witnessed Chairman Brian Mears suffer verbal abuse from one particular supporter who was sitting alongside the Directors' Box.

With less than 20 minutes remaining, winger Clive Walker was introduced and immediately provided Tommy Langley with a goal from his cutback from the left flank at the Shed End.

Kenny Swain then added a second before Walker raced through to net an equaliser.

Then, in the last minute and as at Blackpool eight years earlier, a defender turned in a cross for the winner, the unfortunate player being Sam Allardyce.

WHERE WERE YOU WHEN WE WERE SHOCKING?

The spectator who had previously been heckling Brian Mears then leapt over the barrier to the Directors' box and smothered him in kisses, much to Mrs Mears annoyance.

With the teams reappearing for the second half, we hold out little hope that Chelsea substitute Alan Mayes is likely to have the same impact as Cooke and Walker did in those past memorable triumphs.

Indeed, three more goals are shipped as Fern completes his hat trick and Moore a brace for a 6-0 scoreline.

With time running out, Chelsea are awarded a penalty and after John Bumstead's effort is saved by Rotherham keeper Mountford, the referee orders a retake.

The second attempt is then parried by Mountford to Chris Hutchings who skews the ball wide with the goal at his mercy. It's very much in keeping with the day's events.

It's a long trek home, what with six of us crammed into Bill's Ford Granada. Nobody is prepared to begin an inquest into the dramatic defeat.

However, having completed the journey and back in the pub, the debates begin. The majority feel that Steve Francis should now be preferred to Borota in goal and also the veteran, Colin Viljoen, should be stood down.

We then discuss whose turn it is to drive up to Wigan for the forthcoming midweek League Cup tie. There are no volunteers so we will have to reconvene next Saturday before the home game with Newcastle before a decision is made.

It's not my turn as I have already driven to the defeats at Shrewsbury and Cambridge.

Still 11th in the league but perhaps a League Cup run is on as Wigan Athletic are a division below us.

It might just be our year to reach Wembley again!

Shrewsbury Town 2 Chelsea 2
23rd August 1980

Football League Division Two
Gay Meadow
Chelsea; Petar Borota, Graham Wilkins, Dennis Rofe,
John Bumstead, Micky Droy, Gary Chivers, Ian Britton,
Mike Fillery, Gary Johnson (Peter Rhoades-Brown), Clive
Walker, Mike Nutton
Scorers; Walker 16, Fillery 31
Manager; Geoff Hurst
Referee; Michael Lowe
Attendance; 7,370

It's August Bank Holiday weekend and I have managed to
get Friday off to join up with Bill, Gary, Steve and Ginge
to head up the M40/M42 to Shropshire.

From the pages of the *Good Beer Guide*, Ginge has located a
micro-brewery, the Three Tuns at Bishops Castle, which is
holding a festival over the holiday period.

Furthermore, Bill has always informed us that he is an
experienced camper and amongst the luggage in his motor
is a four-man tent and associated camping accessories.

Whilst we are scheduled to arrive at Green's Caravan and
Camping park at Wentnor in the early afternoon, Mick,
Nick and Tony will join up with us in the evening
journeying up after work.

Upon arrival and after checking in at Green's, we espy the Crown Inn at the top of the hill and decide that we may just have time for a quick pint before erecting the tent.

After sampling a couple of the local ales, we are informed that food is available and tuck into a hearty luncheon of steak and kidney pudding and veg.

With the afternoon disappearing fast, it seems that there may well be an extension of the licensing hours.

Upon enquiry, Norman, our new friend and genial proprietor, informs us that the inn will remain open all afternoon into the evening as it is not only 'market day' but also the *Festival of Flowers* weekend.

Whilst the lads welcome this unexpected news and single out those who have yet to buy a round of drinks, I remind them that it is a trek of almost a mile down the winding hill road where the tent requires erection.

Bill tries to allay my obvious concerns around achieving a comfortable night's sleep mentioning that on previous holiday jaunts together with his wife and two small children, they have had no such problem getting the tent up although the last trip was two years ago!

"If we all pull together then we'll have it up in no time," he advises.

With Mick's car load expected at around 7pm, we head back down the hill and unpack the canvas and poles and try to take in Bill's instructions.

Much to the amusement of the other assembled campers, after an hour of toil and sweat the tent is up... just about.

WHERE WERE YOU WHEN WE WERE SHOCKING?

Soon after the others arrive and, upon learning of the fare on offer at the Crown, head straight back up the hill.

Nobody seems to care too much about how seven people will be able to be accommodated in the four man tent.

When Norman the landlord learns that we are Chelsea supporters, he mentions that one of his young customers by the name of Clarence is "the only Chelsea fan in the village" and will obviously be only too pleased to make our acquaintance when he drops in and perhaps cadge a lift to the game tomorrow.

Come closing time, there is no sign of Clarence but the locals have delighted in trouncing us at the dartboard and bar billiards table.

Enquiries as to the locations of a night club, Chinese takeaway or fish and chip shop are met with raucous laughter.

Norman sells us a couple of flagons of locally produced cider and a box of crisps as we head back to the camping site.

Mick will not be dissuaded from leaving his Ford Mexico at the Crown and offers to ferry us back in two trips. Five of us decide that it will be safer to walk but he insists he'll be alright to drive.

Steve jumps in with Mick whilst the rest of us begin our descent.

Halfway down the hill, we hear a screech of brakes and a loud thud and soon Mick appears walking back towards us. The car is in a ditch with a wheel arch inverted.

Ginge is relieved to find upon opening the passenger door that the cider is intact and Steve has, as yet, not quaffed any.

A gate post is upended and put to good use when the wheel arch is restored to its correct position.

Back at the site, the two flagons are soon emptied and after a polite request from an adjoining tent we decide to turn in. Steve and Mick decide to kip in the battered Ford Mexico.

Waking next morning and viewing the picturesque surroundings, we note that the large tent opposite has a number of Harley Davidson motorcycles parked adjacent to it but we have yet to meet our fellow campers.

On the way to the game, we pop into the Crown Inn but there is no sign of Clarence.

Norman has heard of the encounter with the ditch last night and makes an earnest plea for good behaviour at the game and upon our return this evening.

Arriving at Gay Meadow, we take up our seats in the front row of the main stand.

We are right behind the Chelsea dugout and Bill is soon giving tactical advice to manager Geoff Hurst and his assistant Bobby Gould.

This is our third game of the season. On the opening day a late Mike Fillery header salvaged a point in a 2-2 home draw with Wrexham after the visitors had twice led.

In midweek we went down 2-3 to Derby at the Baseball ground so we are looking for our first win.

WHERE WERE YOU WHEN WE WERE SHOCKING?

The locals are quick to remind us that last season Shrewsbury completed a notable double over us winning this fixture 3-0 before departing the Bridge with a 4-2 victory.

As Shrewsbury wear a yellow and blue kit, Chelsea are sporting an all white strip which I much prefer to the red and white worn here in that drubbing last season.

We begin brightly and soon Clive Walker races clear on the left and fires home. We are still celebrating when Shrewsbury net an equaliser. The Tannoy informs us that the scorer is Atkins.

After half an hour, the hosts fail to clear a corner and Mike Fillery blasts a rising left foot effort into the roof of the net.

We are a happy throng at half time and join Micky Greenaway in a rendition of *One Man Went to Mow* and upon his instruction jump to our feet once *ten men* is achieved.

This seems a fitting song as we are playing at Gay Meadow. I wonder if it will catch on?

In the second half, Chelsea spurn several chances to increase the lead and soon after the home keeper Wardle makes a great save from a John Bumstead header, Shrewsbury equalise through Biggins.

With time running out, the referee approaches the dugout and lectures Bobby Gould for inappropriate touchline coaching and threatens to remove him to the stand.

Bill immediately takes his opportunity to recommend that he replace Gould on the bench much to the amusement of the police and stewards around us but is shepherded back into his seat just before the final whistle.

So three games played and only two points on the board. I really don't fancy the midweek trip to Cardiff for the League Cup tie on Wednesday.

We now head over to the Three Tuns Brewery at Bishops Castle for the evening and I remind the others of Norman's request concerning etiquette when they threaten to disrupt the Morris dancing by joining in.

Come the end of the evening and the lads decide almost unanimously that 'Clerics Cure' has beaten 'Solstice' into second place in the real ale stakes.

It's a much quieter party that arrives back at the campsite given the exertions of the day and the night before.

In the morning, we make the acquaintance of the bikers camped alongside us and learn that they are a Birmingham based chapter of the Hells Angels.

We find common ground in that they too have sampled the real ales at the Tuns and were not impressed by the Morris dancing.

When the conversation turns to music, Steve and Mick are soon discussing with 'Chopper' their favourite rock albums and gigs. I cannot join in as, apart from Kiss and Black Sabbath, I have no other knowledge of the subject matter.

Chopper and his mates profess to having no interest in the beautiful game but understand that Chelsea Football Club, like their own institution, have a fearsome cult following.

As the 'peace-pipe' is passed around the campfire both

groups learn more about the other – their motives, hopes and aspirations.

I am taken aback when they produce newspaper articles and other documentation supporting the monies their association has raised for both national and local charities.

Parting company, we agree not to judge each other by what we read in the newspapers.

Bidding farewell to Norman at the Crown, we finally meet Clarence.

In our brief conversation however, I soon learn that 'the only Chelsea fan in the village' was not aware that 'his team' were playing locally and that an entertaining 2-2 draw took place.

Nought as queer as folk as they say... and don't judge a book by it's cover.

QPR at home next Saturday maybe I will go to Cardiff midweek once I have checked my bank balance upon my return to work on Tuesday.

That first win of the season can't be far off?

Tottenham Hotspur 2 Chelsea 0
April 19th 1975

Football League Division One
White Hart Lane
Chelsea; John Phillips, Gary Locke, John Sparrow, Ian Britton, Micky Droy, Ron Harris, David Hay, Ray Wilkins, Teddy Maybank, Ian Hutchinson, Charlie Cooke
Booked; Locke
Sub Not Used; Steve Kember
Manager; Eddie McCreadie
Referee; Jack K Taylor
Attendance; 51,064

Last Saturday's 0-1 home defeat to Manchester City must go down as the worst performance from a Chelsea team I have witnessed since my first visit to Stamford Bridge in April 1966.

Not one worthy attempt on target in 90 minutes. We now occupy nineteenth position on 31 points one ahead of both Luton Town and Spurs. Carlisle are bottom with 26 points.

Ahead of us are Arsenal and Birmingham City both on 34 points, so with three games remaining it looks like it's going to go to the wire and two of Chelsea, Spurs and Luton will face the drop with the Cumbrians.

Following on from last Saturday's debacle, interim manager Ron Suart who took charge of the team's affairs after Dave Sexton's sacking eleven games into the season last September, requested that Scotland release both Charlie Cooke and David Hay from their squad to face Sweden in midweek, bearing in mind the importance of the club's weekend fixture at White Hart Lane.

Whilst this request was granted, a similar plea to the Welsh FA for the release of goalkeeper John Phillips was turned aside and he played against Hungary.

On Monday, Chelsea played at Fulham in a friendly against the FA Cup finalists, arranged in memory of PC Stephen Tibble who, some months earlier, was shot dead when apprehending an IRA suspect locally.

A crowd of over 12,000 witnessed Chelsea run out 1-0 winners, the goal coming via 18 year old Teddy Maybank who impressed up front alongside Ian Hutchinson.

Following the game, we learned that former Blues favourite Eddie McCreadie has been promoted from the coaching staff and will now replace Stuart as team manager.

Much to my mother's annoyance, Thursday and Friday evenings were punctuated with incoming phone calls from travelling companions calling to confirm our itineraries for Saturday.

On the day of the game and meeting up with my friends at Uxbridge tube station at 10.30, there's already an atmosphere, with Chelsea and Spurs fans grouping together and eyeing the others movements.

We head off to Victoria to meet up with brothers Ralph, Roger and Peter Jones together with Trevor Ingarfill, fellow Chelsea Shed boys, who are travelling up for the game from Orpington in Kent.

Unfortunately, we soon learn of a signal failure upon South East Rail and with the time approaching one o'clock, decide that we cannot wait any longer for our mates as there is every indication that the game will be attended by a capacity crowd of over 50,000 and the gates will be closed well before the 3pm kick off.

Upon boarding a packed underground train, we espy many known Chelsea faces from the likes of Stockwell, Pimlico and Battersea but, again, there's any eerie silence.

Alighting at Seven Sisters, we make our way out onto the High Road for the mile walk up to the ground. Within yards, we are met with the sight of broken shop windows and former Spurs player Dave Mackay's retail outlet "Mackay's Ties" is boarded up with planks of wood.

We are unsure whether the shop has been vandalised or, as in previous years, has been protected as a precautionary matter.

Nearing White Hart Lane, the atmosphere is becoming more tense by the second.

Fans with blooded faces are receiving medical attention at ambulances and the police are overstretched restraining others and endeavouring to place miscreants into their vehicles.

Passing the Corner Pin Pub, police with loudhailers announce that the Park Lane End entrances are now closed and we race around to the Shelf side to gain admission.

We take up a central position on the steep terracing in a

similar place to where I saw Chelsea beat Watford 5-1 on my first visit to Tottenham as a 14 year old when I attended the 1970 FA Cup Semi-Final in 1970.

On that day, three quarters of the crowd appeared to be sporting blue and white with Watford's followers occupying only the Paxton Road end to our right.

In last season's corresponding fixture, a crowd of only 23,000 saw Chelsea overturn a half time deficit to record a 2-1 win with goals from Micky Droy, his first for the club, and Ron Harris.

That was a midweek evening game towards the end of the season with only local bragging rights at stake, unlike today with both clubs fighting to avoid relegation.

Surveying the two ends of the ground at around 2.30 and neither set of supporters are yet to announce themselves until all eyes turn to the right of the Paxton Road End where a sizeable Chelsea contingent endeavour to force their way onto that terrace.

At this point, the Spurs fans – already crammed into that end – attempt to confront them and begin fighting the local constabulary with a number of police helmets finding their way onto the pitch.

It then becomes evident that the larger part of the Park Lane terrace to our left, as in previous seasons, is housing the bulk of the visiting support.

With the Paxton Road rammed to capacity, the Chelsea mob in the corner of that terrace are evacuated onto the pitch perimeter and begin to make their way to join their allies in the Park Lane.

With the police still battling to keep control at the Paxton Road end, hundreds of youths from all four sides of the ground enter the playing area and a number of skirmishes take place although it is unclear as to the allegiances of the pitch invaders.

With kick-off time approaching, the teams appear with referee Jack Taylor racing around the pitch demanding that all the young trespassers return to the terraces with those on the Shelf Side baying *Off, Off, Off!*

We now observe that Eddie McCreadie has stood down experienced former team mates John Hollins and Steve Kember and promoted 18 year old Ray Wilkins to team captain.

Maybank is handed his debut and the Chelsea side also includes 17 year old left back John Sparrow alongside Gary Locke (21) and Ian Britton (20).

Chelsea enjoy the early exchanges and Pat Jennings is called upon to make crucial saves from Britton and an Ian Hutchinson header.

After some 20 minutes, an effort from Charlie Cooke is harshly ruled out by referee Taylor who believes he handled before firing past Jennings.

At half time, with no score, Chelsea have had the lion's share of possession with Spurs yet to trouble John Phillips.

With over an hour played a draw looks likely before disaster strikes when Spurs young skipper Steve Perryman emerges into the penalty area and nets in a rare attack.

Chelsea are quick to respond and when a corner is only half cleared Droy's scrambled effort deflects off two defenders into the net.

However, Jack Taylor again rules against a goal for some infringement which is unclear and a mystery to all around us Spurs and Chelsea supporters alike.

Minutes later Jennings, under pressure from Maybank, fumbles a cross from Cooke into the path of Wilkins but the young captain skews his shot yards wide of a gaping goal much to the horror of the Chelsea hordes assembled in the Park Lane.

After coming so close to salvaging a point Scottish International Alfie Conn nets a second for Spurs and our misery is complete.

It's a long trek back up to Seven Sisters tube station and we move quickly leaving the angry mobs and sounds of police sirens wailing behind us.

Back at Uxbridge, I pick up a copy of the *Evening News* and survey the damage from the stop-press.

The two points Spurs have earned today have taken them one in front of us whilst Luton Town have triumphed 4-1 at Birmingham.

Only Carlisle United, 1-0 winners against Wolves, are below us.

We have two games left, both at home, starting midweek with Sheffield United and then Everton next Saturday.

Spurs visit Arsenal next Saturday before entertaining European Cup finalists Leeds United.

No doubt Arsenal will wish to inflict a crucial defeat on

their hated local rivals but will Leeds play a weakened side before facing Bayern Munich in Paris?

More importantly, can we obtain maximum points from our two remaining games after having won only four at home all season?

Will Eddie McCreadie recall Hollins and Kember or stick with the youngsters he blooded today?

The next seven days are going to be of significant importance to the future of the club bearing in mind the parlous financial situation we find ourselves in.

Relegation is just unthinkable.

COME ON YOU BLUES!

Viktoria Zizkov 0 Chelsea 0
29th September 1994

European Cup Winners Cup Round 1 (2nd Leg)
Strelnice Stadium
Chelsea; Dmitri Kharine, Steve Clarke, Erland Johnsen, Frank Sinclair, Paul Furlong, Gavin Peacock, Dennis Wise, Eddie Newton, David Rocastle, Anthony Barness, Graham Rix
Booked; Wise 56, Kharine 87
Subs Not Used; Michael Duberry, Paul Hughes, Scott Minto, Neil Shipperley, Kevin Hitchcock
Manager; Glenn Hoddle
Referee; Gianni Beschin
Attendance; 5,176

After the disappointment of losing our first FA Cup Final in 24 years last May, we are rewarded with a place in the European Cup Winners' Cup as our nemesis, Manchester United, completed the domestic Double and therefore will compete in the European Champions Cup.

I have always been envious of my peers who over the years have related to me their memories of seeing Chelsea triumph over the mighty Real Madrid in the same competition in Athens in 1971 and visits to the likes of Sofia and Bruges en route to the final.

Just about every Chelsea supporter I know has vowed to follow the team into Europe this season being fearful that it may be another 20 odd years before this happens again!

I was in the office when the draw was made but achieved very little as I spent several hours after 11 o'clock fielding telephone calls from colleagues asking where the town of Zizkov is situated.

Similarly the next few days were taken up formulating provisional travel itineraries and badgering the club offices for details around ticket allocations etc.

It was not long before the travel pages of the *London Evening News* were advertising charter trips to Prague and flyers were being handed out along the Fulham Road at home games detailing excursions separate from those offered by the club.

Most of my would-be travelling companions felt ill at ease to part with monies to the travel operators who, upon enquiry, did not provide cast-iron assurances that they had access to tickets for the game.

I contacted one such advertiser, Prime Events, and was surprised to speak to the proprietor, Mike Ross, whose acquaintance I had made in 1980 when following England in the European Championships in Italy.

Astonishingly, not only did he remember me, but also my travelling companions and which teams we supported.

Mike, at that time, ran his own 'company' called Trans Euro Tours and we had spent two weeks travelling around Italy taking in Milan, Turin, Naples and Rome.

The experience was made all the more interesting when some hotels along the way cancelled his reservations amid the ensuing outbreaks of violence witnessed at England's games with Belgium and the hosts Italy.

WHERE WERE YOU WHEN WE WERE SHOCKING?

After England's elimination at the group stage, we had stayed on to see the final West Germany versus Belgium in Rome.

When our original booking was cancelled, Mike managed to secure accommodation in a 5 star hotel, where among others, England International Dave Watson and his family were holidaying and Kevin Keegan's brother was spending his honeymoon.

Whilst I was pleased to meet the Watson family, I could not quite understand why my companions wished to be photographed with Keegan.

Mike Ross was quick to reassure me that he had contacts in Prague and that obtaining tickets would not be a problem.

However, upon enquiry it appeared that Prime Events had yet to attain any ABTA or IATA accreditation, had yet to be incorporated at Companies House and did not have access to credit card acceptance facilities!

Despite all these downsides, the very fact that Mike remembered me after some 14 years swayed my judgement and I decided to rush a cheque off to him to secure a place on a three day excursion.

Upon hearing of my former dealings with Mike, and having committed my hard earned cash to him, five of my regular travelling companions decided to follow suit.

Over the next few days I was plagued with phone-calls from them after the announcement that the match would not be played in Prague but in Jablonec some 60 miles north near the Polish border.

Again, I received verbal assurances from Mike that this did not cause any problem although we may have to pay another ten or twenty pounds for the provision of coach travel on the day of the game.

After relaying this information to the lads and allaying their fears, I then remembered that when I travelled with Trans Euro in 1980 we had stayed on the southern coast of Italy in the small resort of Varazze and travelled up to the England versus Belgium game in Turin by coach on the day of the game. Returning in the evening, we learned that whilst our excursion had gone okay another 60 or so England supporters had been left stranded in Varazze when a further two coaches failed to appear.

Mike had blamed the Italian coach operators at the time but I thought it best not to relay this episode to those travelling to Prague.

We depart Heathrow Tuesday tea-time, arriving Prague late evening with Wednesday for sightseeing and the game Thursday returning Friday morning.

Upon arrival in Prague, we make our way to the coach which is to transport us to our budget hotel. After about an hour our driver pulls up and, we assume, asks for directions from a local.

Thankfully however, we soon arrive and find we are obviously a long way from the capital. As it is nearing midnight, all present are content to hit the hotel bar and it's not long before the management are recommending that we retire for the night after a few Chelsea anthems have boomed out.

Venturing out on Wednesday morning, we find that we are a bus and tube ride from the centre of Prague but conquer the language barrier and are soon enjoying the sights.

Upon returning to the hotel in the evening, we meet up with those in our group and also others we only met last night.

Exchanging stories of our visits to Prague during the day, we hear that renowned Chelsea 'face' Stephen Hickmott has made the journey from his new home in Thailand and was spotted in the Sports Bar.

There are also rumours that fans of Sparta Prague are targeting Chelsea followers with a view to a confrontation in the capital after the game tomorrow evening.

On Thursday morning, Mike Ross meets us in the hotel reception and I am relieved that we shall only require one coach which is already parked outside.

He informs me that he has the match tickets with him and that they will be distributed when we near Jablonec.

Once we are in the vicinity of the ground, the tickets are indeed handed out but some of our number are uncomfortable that they bear an inscription reading, "Not valid in the possession of Chelsea supporters".

Mike allays any fears around accessing the ground though mentioning that he has an interpreter with him who will escort all of us through the turnstiles.

Alighting the coach, there's a dark and sombre atmosphere. It's hard to distinguish between the ranks of armed police in different coloured uniforms. A military tank would not seem out of place with the surroundings.

We make our way past smoking burly policewomen who

are restraining their muzzled bullmastiff hounds.

The Strelnice stadium resembles an English non-league ground surrounded by forest.

Thankfully, we are soon through the turnstile and make our way to the main stand.

The majority of the Chelsea support is housed upon the standing terrace to our left which is interspersed with trees.

Their number swells to perhaps 1,000 when we see a couple of hundred alight from the club's official coaches in the nearby car park and race to enter the ground five minutes into the game.

Jim delights in our fellow supporters' late arrival and enquires whether they were delayed in Preston or Dresden.

Casting my eyes over the insignia in front of the Chelsea followers, I note that amongst the banners and flags proclaiming support from the likes of Battersea, Brixton, Tunbridge Wells and Slough, there is also a banner seemingly declaring the presence of a politically motivated group of the club's supporters.

We hold a 4-2 lead from the first leg at Stamford Bridge a couple of weeks ago when our goal scorers were Paul Furlong, Frank Sinclair, David Rocastle and Dennis Wise.

I believe that this to be the first time that three black players had netted for Chelsea in one game. Today though, we are missing a few players through injury or illness.

Youth team coach and former England International Graham Rix is making his full Chelsea debut a few weeks before his 37th birthday.

The first half an hour passes without incident before Anthony Barness playing only his third game in three seasons brings down Majoros and a penalty is awarded.

To our relief, Dmitri Kharine makes a fine save from Vabrec and the follow up from Poborsky. A few minutes later, Zizkov have a scrambled effort from Jancula ruled out for an infringement.

The second half is forgettable affair with only a long range free kick from Wise troubling their keeper. In an effort to stir their team into action, the Tannoy system belts out recorded crowd noise but to little effect.

The attendance can only be about 5,000 with about half being Chelsea supporters.

The only further entertainment comes when the stadium announcer confirms a booking for Kharine for time wasting and adds that he (Kharine) is from "Chelsea in London".

At the end of the game, a goalless draw takes us through to the next round.

Chelsea Chairman Ken Bates is sat a few rows in front of us and is subject to a few catcalls concerning our ability to obtain entry to the game when he had stated that it would not be possible and he is also mocked as to the late arrival of those on the official club excursion.

We return to the coach park and take up our seats ready to depart for Prague.

Sitting near the back of the coach, I notice there is some sort of commotion at the front and people are urging the driver to keep the door closed.

As we depart, I observe a group of youths through the window pointedly making threatening gestures at some of my fellow passengers.

Having followed Chelsea for some 25 years I do not recognise any of their faces from my travels.

Much of the return journey is in silence and we are unsure exactly what took place at the front of the vehicle at the time of departure.

Alighting back in the centre of Prague, our group head for refreshment.

At the bar, people are discussing the apparent polarisation of two sections of the Chelsea support as well as what turned out to be a near fatal attack previously described which had taken place on the coach as they left the ground.

This incident follows a fracas on the opening day of the season when, following our 2-0 home win over Norwich City and according to some reports, two opposing groups of 'politically-minded' Chelsea supporters were involved in another violent confrontation resulting in several requiring hospital treatment.

Having looked forward to this trip for some weeks and enjoyed the sights and the company this occurrence has left a very bad taste in my mouth.

Arriving home Friday morning I put the radio on and learn that in the next round of the competition Chelsea have been drawn to play Austria Vienna.

Before catching up on much needed sleep I make a call to the office to secure the days off required to make the next jaunt into Europe.

Whilst these are indeed exciting times following our team, I am fearful of further clashes between rival factions purporting to have the interest of Chelsea Football Club at heart.

Just who are they and what are their objectives?

Perhaps things will become clearer by the time I call Mike Ross at Prime Events to discuss his packages for Vienna.

Wrexham 2 Chelsea 0
29th December 1979

Football League Division 2
Racecourse Ground
Chelsea; Petar Borota, Gary Locke, John Sparrow, John Bumstead, Micky Droy, Gary Chivers, Ian Britton, Mike Fillery, Tommy Langley, Clive Walker, Ron Harris (Peter Rhoades-Brown 64)
Manager; Geoff Hurst
Referee; George Flint
Attendance; 15,641

After defeating Leicester City 1-0 with a goal from Mike Fillery at the Bridge on Boxing Day we are now in second place. Looking back over the first half of the season we have seen spells of indifferent form and changes in staff and playing personnel.

After the first five matches had resulted in two wins, two defeats and a draw, manager Danny Blanchflower was replaced by former England forward Geoff Hurst.

Blanchflower's departure followed a 1-2 home defeat to Birmingham a game which also saw the last appearances in Chelsea blue of the legendary Peter Osgood and the much maligned Trevor Aylott.

Whilst Hurst's first game in charge was a 0-3 reverse at lowly Shrewsbury, the team then went on to record five successive victories before suffering back to back defeats at home to Fulham and away at Sunderland.

Thereafter another fine run of five wins began with a 7-3 thrashing of Orient at Brisbane Road with Lee Frost netting a hat-trick, Clive Walker a brace and Fillery and Ian Britton one apiece.

Meeting up at Euston, Bill has brought the leftovers from his party last night. No turkey sandwiches just beer and spirits.

When I approach an elderly newspaper vendor for some reading material, we exchange compliments of the season before he enquires as to my destination. I tell him that I am going to Wrexham via Chester.

He then points to two other gentlemen nearby and, in a whispered voice, informs me that they are plain clothed police officers making the same journey.

Alighting at Chester we check the train times for the onward connection and decide that we have time to visit a local hostelry.

Once assembled at the bar, we see from the window the two policemen crossing the road towards us before they enter the premises.

After they order their soft drinks, we decide to make a hasty retreat back into the station and after a few minutes espy the officers trailing us once more.

Whilst there is a ten minute delay before our scheduled departure to Wrexham, there is a train approaching for Liverpool.

The six of us board the Liverpool train and peer out of the window at our pursuers who enter the adjoining carriage.

Just as the train is about to depart, we jump out back onto the platform but the policemen take similar action and we are all then heading for the Wrexham train.

Taking up a compartment, the officers then appear in the corridor and we beckon them in to join us.

Smilingly, they admit defeat in our game of hide and seek and relax in the knowledge that we do not have any agenda involving hooliganism or violence.

One of the officers informs us that he is a follower of Charlton Athletic and relates tales of woe from his times supporting them, so much so that we cannot reach Wrexham soon enough to escape the doom and gloom he relates to us.

Regrettably, I didn't obtain seats in advance for this game and, what with it being the festive period, my funds were somewhat limited. So we pay at the turnstile and enter the terracing behind the goal.

The view of the playing area has to be the worst I have ever experienced as the terrace is actually below pitch level and my eyes were just about in line with the playing surface.

To make matters even worse, the action has to be viewed through an eight-foot high fence.

Despite Wrexham's lowly league position, they make all the early running as indeed they did in the game at Stamford Bridge back in August before late goals from Ian Britton and John Bumstead sealed a 3-1 win.

In the 13th minute, local hero Dixie McNeil fires Wrexham ahead although quite how, I am unsure as the view is appalling.

I decide an early comfort break is in order and fight my way out to the back of the terrace.

When a matchday steward enquires as to the scorer, I reply that given the atrocious view and facilities generally I do not know nor care and request that he allows me to exit the game as I would rather go to the pub.

Quite to my astonishment, the steward then offers to unlock a padlocked gate which offers access to paddock terracing upon the side where there is an acceptable view and no fencing.

I then ask that he waits whilst I alert my five travelling companions and amazingly we are soon relocated.

However, within five minutes of us being in our new surroundings, some disgruntled locals bring our presence to the attention of another less sympathetic steward who summons police assistance and we are frogmarched around the pitch perimeter and unceremoniously bundled back into our pen.

On the pitch, nothing is improving for us and it is no surprise when Mick Vinter nets a second for the hosts.

With time running out, Chelsea bring on young attacking winger Peter Rhoades-Brown for his debut in place of Ron Harris. However, despite the youngster's sterling efforts, we are well beaten. The long train journey back is a silent and sober affair as we learn that we have dropped a place in the league to third.

Back at Euston, Bill persuades us all to return to Walton-on-Thames for another festive shindig and we all accept his kind invitation.

Arriving at his home however, the mood changes when we are greeted by his wife who has just witnessed viewing our earlier excursion around the pitch on *Match of the Day*.

After assuring her that her husband will not be returning to North Wales for a future court hearing the party is soon in full swing.

We discuss our itinerary for the New Year's Day trip to fellow promotion seekers Luton Town and our chances in the FA Cup with a home tie against 4th Division Wigan Athletic scheduled for next Saturday.

Yes… 1980 could just be our year!

York City 2 Chelsea 2
24th April 1976

Football League Division Two
Bootham Crescent
Chelsea; John Phillips, Ron Harris, Graham Wilkins (Brian Bason), Garry Stanley, Steve Wicks, David Hay, Ian Britton, Ray Wilkins, Steve Finnieston, Ken Swain, Bill Garner
Scorers; Britton 64 (Pen), Finnieston 86
Booked; Britton, Ray Wilkins
Manager; Eddie McCreadie
Referee; Anthony E Morrissey
Attendance; 4,914

We come to the end of a long season and our final game is a return to Bootham Crescent York where we enjoyed a 2-0 fourth round FA Cup victory back in January.

After last season's relegation from the First Division, we had hoped to make a swift return to the top flight however it looks like we shall finish mid-table in 11th position.

Today, I have chosen to travel upon the 'Football Special', the club charter train from Kings Cross. Earlier in the season, British Rail had suspended these excursions after outbreaks of hooliganism, notably following our 0-3 defeat at Luton Town in August.

However, during the suspension, Chelsea stalwart and British Rail booking clerk Micky Greenaway had successfully commandeered excursions to the likes of Oldham, Blackpool and Hull for several hundred likeminded die hards to attend matches.

Upon the opening day of the season, I travelled upon one of two special trains to Sunderland. Each train accommodated around 600 Chelsea followers.

Upon alighting at Seaburn, our thousand plus contingent were escorted to Roker Park by the local constabulary, passing the ranks of the baying Sunderland fans at the rear of the home Fulwell End. Arriving at the opposite Roker End, it soon became apparent that the home support were also in occupation in their thousands.

We made our way up the stairs to the left of the terracing with the police struggling to keep the rival factions apart and missiles raining down upon us.

Once assembled 'the thin blue line' managed to keep order for most of the game in which Bill Garner gave Chelsea a first half lead from some 25 yards only for goalkeeper Steve Sherwood to gift an equaliser to the veteran Bryan 'Pop' Robson just before the interval.

Shortly before the end, Dennis Longhorn netted the winner for the hosts with a screaming 20 yard shot at the Fulwell End.

At that point, the Chelsea following – upon the instruction of Daniel Harkins and 'Babs' – moved to the top right of the terracing to beat our retreat to the exits nearer to the road back to Seaburn station.

Once more, the Sunderland fans began leaving and assembled by the exits below and once more, the police cordons thwarted a major confrontation.

Viewing the Wearside element below from the upper terracing, a younger Chelsea follower, Stephen Hickmott, advanced onto a crash barrier and proclaimed that our following was superior to that of the home side and that we had nothing to fear when venturing out onto the streets outside.

His rallying cry was indeed heeded and soon after the Sunderland hordes dispersed amidst the sounds of breaking glass, baying hounds and police sirens.

Unfortunately, the football special upon which I was a passenger broke down on the return journey at St. Neots in Cambridgeshire and, after arriving back at 1am into London, I had to board a paper train from Paddington to Slough at dawn and then walk some eight miles home.

Unperturbed by the opening day defeat however, I still made the following mid-week trip to West Bromwich Albion where Chelsea earned their first point of the season in a goalless draw.

Whilst our youngsters have shown immense promise at times, particularly in the first two home games when Carlisle and Oxford were both beaten 3-1, some of our away results have been hard to bear.

In September, the club suffered the ignominy of defeats at Crewe Alexandra, in the League Cup, and at Oldham Athletic in the space of four days.

Many of our followers, some who only four years earlier had witnessed the club winning a major European trophy in Athens, were now witnessing losses to teams which we had only been aware of from our pools coupons.

Before this season, despite having achieved an O Level

pass in Geography, I was completely unaware of the location of Crewe or Oldham.

In early October we travelled to Southampton and were defeated 4-1 this being a particularly bitter pill to swallow as former Chelsea legend, Peter Osgood, was now plying his trade for the Saints and whilst he didn't score against us, he was instrumental in assisting in the third and fourth goals.

There was though an upturn in form after the defeat at the Dell with the team reaching eighth position by the end of November after consecutive away wins at Hull City, Blackpool and Bristol Rovers.

Also during this period, Chelsea drew 2-2 with Plymouth Argyle at Stamford Bridge in a game I will always remember as first, Peter Bonetti made as good a save as any I can ever remember from a Paul Mariner header and secondly, Ray Wilkins scored with a magnificent diving header whilst almost horizontal around the penalty spot at the Shed End.

However, early December saw us beaten 1-0 at home by promotion seeking Bolton Wanderers when Ray Wilkins saw his penalty saved by Barry Siddall before another defeat on formerly unchartered territory 2-1 at Carlisle United.

The Saturday before Christmas witnessed top of the table Sunderland's visit with many of those who had travelled to Wearside on the opening day now taking up their customary position in the North Stand.

Whilst the previous home games against Plymouth and Bolton had seen spasmodic outbreaks of disorder prior to kick-off, trouble flared throughout the whole match much like at Roker Park back in August.

Thankfully, Chelsea extracted sweet revenge for their opening day defeat when the diminutive Scot Ian Britton volleyed home with some fifteen minutes remaining.

On Boxing Day, Chelsea travelled to east London and were surprisingly beaten 3-1 by Orient after Teddy Maybank had seemingly rescued a point when equalising with some ten minutes remaining, only for the home side to net late goals from Bennett and Cunningham.

Just twenty four hours later, Chelsea slipped to thirteenth position when going down 2-3 at home to Charlton Athletic for whom Derek Hales scored twice.

With our promotion bid looking doomed, all eyes then turned to the forthcoming 3rd Round FA Cup tie with Bristol Rovers at the Bridge.

In view of the club's well documented financial crisis, a request to play the game on New Year's Day instead of the following Saturday was agreed, and a crowd of over 35,000 witnessed a 1-1 draw.

Back at Eastville two days later, Chelsea recorded a victory as they had done in the league in November this time winning 1-0 with a late goal from the ever improving Kenny Swain.

It would seem that the FA Cup was to become a distraction to the side as our league form became somewhat chequered.

January witnessed home defeats to Oldham Athletic 0-3 and West Bromwich Albion 1-2 however sandwiched inbetween a 3-1 win at Nottingham Forest was maybe our best performance of the season with Charlie Cooke rolling back the years with assists for Bill Garner, Ray Wilkins and Ian Hutchinson.

Our reward for defeating today's opponents in the FA Cup 4th Round was a home tie with Crystal Palace where over 54,000 packed into Stamford Bridge. At the interval Palace led 2-0 with goals from Chatterton and Taylor before Chelsea fought back to level through Ray Wilkins and Steve Wicks.

With some 15 minutes remaining, Peter Taylor netted the winner for the visitors from a free kick at the North Stand end.

However, despite the game being a near classic, it will be largely remembered by those present and the millions who viewed the highlights on BBC *Match of the Day* for the gratuitous violence witnessed on the North Stand terrace.

One youth was seen to adopt the martial art of Kung-Fu when launching an attack on a rival fan and this image would be beamed around the world.

The following Wednesday, a home crowd of only just over 10,000 saw a drab 0-0 draw with Hull City.

Thereafter, once again, our form became inconsistent with further goalless home draws with Bristol Rovers and Fulham but entertaining games at Plymouth in a 3-0 win and a 2-2 draw at promotion chasing Bristol City.

Also, after dominating the game at Bolton when Ian Britton had given us a deserved second half lead, we were defeated 2-1 with first David Hay heading into his own net and then the luckless Graham Wilkins followed suit when misplacing a back-pass to Peter Bonetti.

Making our way from the station to the ground we pass the pub where we escaped the snow back in January. On that day we grouped at the bar around a transistor radio which alerted us to the apparent postponement of the tie.

Upon hearing this news, a minibus of Chelsea followers consulted the newspaper for alternative fixtures and departed en-masse arguing whether to head for Leeds where Crystal Palace were playing or Bradford City who were entertaining non-league Tooting and Mitcham.

A few minutes after their departure, a further announcement upon the radio confirmed that the game was on and had not been postponed.

Hopefully, our fellow supporters would have learned of this news but I wondered whether they learned of our passage to the next round when leaving either Elland Road or Valley Parade!

With York City already relegated, today's attendance is under 5,000, whereas back in January, our following of some 6,000 outnumbered the home support in a crowd of 9,500.

The game indeed has an end of season feel to it and after a scoreless first half, Jimmy Seal puts the hosts ahead, only for Ian Britton to level from the penalty spot a few minutes later.

With time running out, Micky Cave restores York's lead, but Steve 'Jock' Finnieston then races clear to net a second equaliser.

On the train home, a number of presentations are made to the club stewards for their sterling efforts during the season and also to Micky Greenaway for organising excursions during the FA ban.

I turn my thoughts to next season. Whilst goalkeeper Peter Bonetti has been in fine form we can't rely on him being around for many more seasons but deputy John Phillips is also a reliable custodian of the gloves.

Full backs Gary Locke and John Sparrow have shown immense promise and have been capped by England at junior levels, as has centre back Steve Wicks who is forging a great partnership with Scottish International David Hay.

In midfield, young captain Ray Wilkins is expected to gain full England honours soon and Chairman Brian Mears has promised that he, along with all our other promising youngsters, will not be sold to relieve the club's financial burden. Garry Stanley, Ray Lewington and Ian Britton have all attracted media attention for their tireless work in the middle of the park.

Up front, Finnieston has become a consistent goal scorer since returning from injury and replacing Teddy Maybank who has not featured since the FA Cup defeat to Crystal Palace.

Kenny Swain complements Finnieston superbly and can also operate wide or in midfield.

As well as them, there is Ron Harris, Bill Garner, Ian Hutchinson, Micky Droy and John Dempsey who bring a wealth of experience to the squad.

Yes, all in all, I am convinced that we are well equipped to make an assault on the Second Division title next season. Can't wait... bring it on!

Real Zaragoza 3 Chelsea 0
April 6th 1995

European Cup Winners Cup (Semi Final 1ˢᵗ Leg)
La Romareda
Chelsea; Kevin Hitchcock, Steve Clarke, Scott Minto, Erland Johnsen, Frank Sinclair, John Spencer (Mark Stein), Paul Furlong, Gavin Peacock, Andy Myers, Nigel Spackman, David Rocastle (Glenn Hoddle)
Booked; Minto
Manager; Glenn Hoddle
Referee; Leif Sundell
Attendance; 35,000

Quite unbelievably, we have made it to the semi-finals of the European Cup Winners' Cup despite our chequered league form which sees us currently in fifteenth position.

However, in many ways this season has been a very different and enjoyable experience when taking in the trips to Prague, Vienna and Bruges.

Many new friendships have been made and others cemented upon the way.

Unfortunately, though each away tie has been played out against a backdrop of anticipated hooliganism not helped by the media who always seem to be waiting with bated breath for any disorder to report on.

We have again opted to entrust the tour company Prime

Events and its proprietor Mike Ross to take us to Zaragoza and back and their package appears very interesting and reasonably priced.

Mike's package involves flying to and from Barcelona via Brussels on Tuesday making our own way by train to Zaragoza on Thursday then back to Barca on Friday and watching the Catalans host Real Sociedad on Sunday evening before flying home Monday.

Budget hotel just off La Ramblas. £280 all in!

On Wednesday evening, having becoming acquainted ourselves with La Ramblas and its surroundings Ian Seymour informs us that he is going to the airport to meet two of our exiled stalwart supporters in Dag Bjune and Dave Suttie and bring them back to our party.

Dag is from Oslo and the same age as myself, 39, and has been a frequent visitor to Stamford Bridge for more than 20 years having fallen in love with the club after watching the 1970 FA Cup Final on Norwegian TV.

He is immediately distinguishable from his flowing blonde locks and when not watching football he fronts and tours with a Cajun band.

Dave now lives in Melbourne but gets back at least twice a season to follow the family tradition of supporting the Blues.

Ron, Dave's father, still travels from Reading for every home game and we recently discovered a photograph of him in a supporters group who had travelled up to Newcastle overnight by coach for a fixture in the mid 1930s.

WHERE WERE YOU WHEN WE WERE SHOCKING?

After sampling the Barcelona night life, I awake to find that we only have an hour to get to the railway station before boarding the express for the four hour journey north.

Making my way along the hotel corridor, I rouse all those in our party to ensure that we make the train.

Peering into Ian's room I note that Dave is still comatose upon the floor and Dag's legs are protruding from the wardrobe!

Unfortunately, a hotel chambermaid has also noted the situation and thankfully is more concerned as to the guests' health than the violation of hotel rules and regulations around room occupancy levels etc.

Miraculously however, within minutes, we are all on our way to the railway terminus.

Our group is about 20 strong and takes up a couple of carriages. Soon after setting off, I'm asked to mind Tom and Kim's baggage whilst they head off in search of the buffet car for possible hangover cures.

After twenty minutes or so, I am the only one left in the carriage and decide to also venture towards the amenities.

Once there and just like the previous evening on Las Ramblas, I find that the party is in full swing. The Chelsea anthems boom out and it hits me that we really are on our way to a major European semi-final tie for the first time in nearly 25 years.

Alighting in Zaragoza around lunchtime, we are met by Mike Ross who assures us that, as in Bruges in the quarter final, our match tickets are in a hotel safe.

Unfortunately though, the local Spanish police are also in attendance and seem Hell bent on returning us to Barcelona and want to see proof of our reservations and tickets.

Mr Ross argues vociferously in their native tongue and at the same time whistles up half a dozen cabs and thankfully the police back off… for now anyway.

And so to the game. We have decent seats in the main stand away from the official Chelsea contingent behind the goal to our right.

Real Zaragoza are fourth in the Spanish League and are soon into their stride.

After only eight minutes, Pardeza heads them into the lead from a corner. Esnaider then adds a second after half an hour and we look jaded in our tangerine and graphite away colours.

Just before the hour mark, Esnaider grabs his second and player manager Glen Hoddle brings himself on in place of David Rocastle and also substitutes John Spencer for Mark Stein.

Sadly, we do not manage an away goal which would give us some hope in the return leg.

The last fifteen minutes are played out against a backdrop of the Spanish police attacking innocent Chelsea supporters with their batons.

0-3 is a fair reflection on proceedings. Zaragoza's number eight, the Uruguayan Gustavo Poyet, basically ran the game but collected a booking which rules him out of the second leg.

WHERE WERE YOU WHEN WE WERE SHOCKING?

The following morning when embarking on the return journey to Barcelona I had a most uplifting experience. Having checked out the itinerary and waiting on the platform an announcement came over the Tannoy in Spanish.

An elderly lady then gestured to three young schoolboys nearby one of whom then approached me to inform that there was a change to the departure platform.

I complimented the youngster and enquired just what the lady had said to him.

He told me that whilst she spoke no other languages it was important that a foreign traveller should be looked after and if they spoke enough English they were to relay the change to me.

Back in Barca on Sunday evening, I experienced the lofty heights of the Nou Camp and found myself not in awe of Stoikov, the home side's centre forward, but wondering if any Chelsea supporters had actually been present when Charlie Cooke made his debut in the 0-5 Inter Cities Fairs Cup semi-final thrashing in 1966.

The game ended 1-1 with Ronald Koeman slicing a cross into his own net in injury time to give Sociedad a point.

Changing aircraft in Brussels on Monday, we were joined by members of the 'glam rock' band Slade minus front man Noddy Holder they having just played a gig there.

Ian Seymour decided that we should all welcome them aboard with a rendition of *Tiger Feet* which indeed we did and the band members – particularly the diminutive Dave Hill – saw the funny side and jigged in the aisle.

Back in Heathrow, I soon discovered that my luggage had gone missing and went about arranging for it to be located and returned to me as soonest. Unfortunately, I did not encounter any kindness as that shown to me by the elderly Spanish lady in Zaragoza railway station.

Arriving back home, there was only time for a quick change of clothes before heading off to Selhurst Park for our evening fixture with Wimbledon.

Before leaving the flat, I scroll down the voice messages stored upon the answer-phone.

Sadly the first is from Steve to let me know that Frank has passed away at the age of 89.

Secondly Cheryl has decided that she will be only too pleased to take up my recent request to accompany me to a game at Stamford Bridge.

One door closes...

GATE 17
THE COMPLETE COLLECTION
(AUGUST 2018)

FOOTBALL

Over Land and Sea - Mark Worrall
Chelsea here, Chelsea There - Kelvin Barker, David Johnstone, Mark Worrall
Chelsea Football Fanzine - the best of cfcuk
One Man Went to Mow - Mark Worrall
Chelsea Chronicles (Five Volume Series) - Mark Worrall
Making History Not Reliving It - Kelvin Barker, David Johnstone, Mark Worrall
Celery! Representing Chelsea in the 1980s - Kelvin Barker
Stuck On You: a year in the life of a Chelsea supporter - Walter Otton
Palpable Discord: a year of drama and dissent at Chelsea - Clayton Beerman
Rhyme and Treason - Carol Ann Wood
Eddie Mac Eddie Mac - Eddie McCreadie's Blue & White Army
The Italian Job: A Chelsea thriller starring Antonio Conte - Mark Worrall
Carefree! Chelsea Chants & Terrace Culture - Mark Worrall, Walter Otton
Diamonds, Dynamos and Devils - Tim Rolls
Arrivederci Antonio: The Italian Job (part two) - Mark Worrall
Where Were You When We Were Shocking? - Neil L. Smith

FICTION

Blue Murder: Chelsea till I die - Mark Worrall
The Wrong Outfit - Al Gregg
The Red Hand Gang - Walter Otton
Coming Clean - Christopher Morgan
This Damnation - Mark Worrall
Poppy - Walter Otton

NON FICTION

Roe2Ro - Walter Otton
Shorts - Walter Otton

www.gate17.co.uk

Printed in Great Britain
by Amazon